Tales of ITT

Tales of ITT

An Insider's Report

THOMAS S. BURNS

Houghton Mifflin Company Boston
1974

FIRST PRINTING   W

Library of Congress Cataloging in Publication Data

Burns, Thomas S
   Tales of ITT; an insider's report.

   1. International Telephone and Telegraph Corpora-
tion.   2. Business and politics—United States.
I.   Title.
HE8846.164B87   384.6'06'273   74–10991
ISBN 0–395–18488–6

Printed in the United States of America

For My Father and Mother,

Contents

Tales of ITT

Introduction

IN THE FALL of 1969 I was wrapping up a general manager assignment, selling off a small cable company, Hitemp Wires. With my home in a Los Angeles suburb and my office in Westbury, Long Island, I felt the urgency to complete the transaction and end the 6000 miles of commuting almost every weekend. The Hitemp situation was what might be described as fluid: while the Long Island Division was being sold to Ametek, a large conglomerate, our parent company was being bought up by Harbill, a small conglomerate. Such activities were in vogue at the time, but personally unsettling.

Then, one bright October day while lunching in Manhattan, I received an invitation from ITT to join their management team. The offer sounded not only fascinating but reasonably secure. There weren't many bigger fish in the sea than ITT, so their chance of being gobbled up was remote. And after some brief discussions with personnel people at ITT World Headquarters in New York, I was

convinced that I was joining the number one gobbler in
the world.

As the tip of the iceberg was revealed, the ITT plan to
build a submarine cable plant in San Diego seemed relatively simple and straightforward. The company owned
about two thirds of the world's submarine cable manufacturing capacity. It would contract to buy the competition, a Western Electric plant in Baltimore, and move the
equipment by ship to San Diego. Once the plant was installed, ITT would have over 50 percent of the submarine
communications and oceanographic cable manufacturing
capability in the United States, and close to a monopoly
worldwide. And that, I was told, was the way that President
Geneen liked to do business: an orderly sort of arrangement
in an industry ruled by a kind of cartel system. Briefly mentioned, without emphasis, was the fact that ITT seldom
built a business of this kind; almost always "going businesses" were acquired. We all learned later on what a difference there is between building and buying companies in
the ITT scheme of things.

A management team was formed from London and
New York. Division Vice Presidents Hayden Moore, Frank
Deighan, and I took up residence at the ITT Defense Space
Group Headquarters in Nutley, New Jersey, and estab-
lished annexes at the ITT World Headquarters in New
York City, San Diego, and Washington, D.C. For the better
part of a year we shuttled back and forth between these
locations. We drafted business plans, chased military and
AT&T cable business, traveled Europe for support from the
ITT cable system, and worked with the ITT staffs and

watch-dog committees responsible for our efforts. When the planning phase ended and construction began we set up permanent offices in San Diego and began the same coast-to-coast commuting schedule I had left the year before.

From the beginning we were made aware in many ways that the Cable Division program was a Geneen pet project. Approvals for large capital outlays were never seriously questioned, the ITT staffs were fretful but seldom critical of our efforts, and ITT's most powerful politicians, inside and outside the company, were at our disposal. It was an exhilarating atmosphere for Cable Division management. We felt we were the swashbuckling adventurers of the cable industry and backed by Geneen's money and power anything was possible.

But gradually came the realization that we were only pawns in a larger and more complex game, the ITT anti-trust battles that were entering a crucial stage. More and more division management became involved with the ITT anti-antitrust skirmishers in Washington through a number of overlapping associations.

As Geneen's pet project we received a disproportionate amount of attention from important lobbyists, and legislators, especially Congressman Bob Wilson from San Diego, who had parlayed his association with Geneen into hotels and other local investments. He was determined to bring a major manufacturing complex into his back yard. ITT needed a close political associate who would insure Administration support in the company's antitrust battles; in Wilson they had the Republican party's chief fund raiser and a close friend of the President. Nixon was a Southern

California son who considered San Diego his "lucky city" and was shopping for a peaceful site for the Republican nominating convention. The areas of mutual interest seemed to fit together very well.

As the Cable Division plans proceeded, our management had access to the technical, marketing, and political assets of our giant parent. Sometimes as observers, sometimes as interested parties, we were privy to the planning processes and political campaigns staged by and for ITT top brass in New York and Washington. We backbenched General Managers' Meetings, prepared and presented business plans before Geneen and his court, and played politics with Bill Merriam's Washington crew of lobbyists. As a vantage point for watching the ITT – Justice Department struggle evolve, our position was ideal. We worked with the ITT players at all levels and had the benefit of their candor and critical comments, most of which would never find their way to ITT World Headquarters or the White House.

In a way, the Cable Division program was one of the casualties of the antitrust war. As political alliances shifted, so did the investment commitments, the business fortunes of the Division. The embarrassments connected with ITT's offer to subsidize the Republican National Convention in San Diego terminated the grandiose, multi-plant schemes. Even the expansionist die-hards finally conceded the scheme unworkable. Today there stands a single plant on the Sweetwater Channel at National City, representing a staggering financial loss never mentioned at ITT Stockholders' Meetings. Plans for future development of the site have been scrapped, although the National City and San

Diego patrons who lobbied in favor of concessions are encouraged by the company's public relations department not to abandon hope.

The ITT campaign to keep the Hartford Insurance Company was successful, but the cost may prove disastrous. Congressional investigations continue, Nader's Raiders nip at the company's heels, and the Watergate investigations are beginning to reveal the patronage and politicking involved in other areas of Administration interest.

When finally it became obvious that the Cable Division program was a failing, politically-motivated adventure and a financial disaster, I ended my association with ITT, intrigued very little by the possibilities of staff positions in Brussels or marketing assignments in New York. Enough, already, of the intrigues, missionary travels, and bruising political battling. Like many ex-ITT executives before me, I opted to rejoin the human race.

Ancient History

I THINK ITT has always been the same. As a young marketeer I remember dealing with the ITT Federal Laboratories, whose reputation for skullduggery and knavery was taken as a matter of fact.

"That's ITT," my boss at General Electric said. While Harold Geneen was transforming the ITT corporate personality, the company was recasting Geneen's management style into a more sinister mold. The company's history is divided into the Behn and Geneen eras, but really there is a commonality of business philosophy that has flowed uninterrupted since the early days of the first South American telephones.

The International Telephone & Telegraph Company was founded in 1920 by Sosthenes Behn, a business adventurer in the grand style. Undercapitalized Puerto Rican businessmen had started a telephone company, and Behn, then a struggling sugar broker, picked up the pieces when the founders became insolvent. He recognized the possibilities of the infant telephone industry at a time when few others would gamble on its shaky technical future. Sosthenes and his brother Hernand became the new management and named the company International Telephone & Telegraph Corporation, close enough to be confused with the giant American Telephone & Telegraph Corporation. Like RCA, Sylvania, and the other companies struggling to survive in the early days of electronics and wireless communications, ITT hung on to AT&T coattails and waited for the partition of the industry that was certain to come. They knew that AT&T would become too big to suit the trust-busters in Congress.

Most companies were content to wait for that great day and meanwhile take the crumbs that fell from the AT&T groaning board. But Behn wanted more from the first. In the early 1920's he began an expansion, independent of AT&T, to link up the first of ITT's European systems. When AT&T's major subsidiary, Western Electric Company, was forced to split off its international arm in 1925, Behn was ready.

Although AT&T and ITT have been covertly carving up the communications world ever since, they continually seem to be at war in a confusion of interest and policies, and no quarter is ever asked or given.

Behn continued his telecommunications expansion and took over total control of ITT when his brother died. In 1933 he formed Standard Elektrizitäts Gesellschaft (SEG) in Germany and in doing so linked ITT with the Nazi movement. Behn rationalized his consorting with the Nazis as simply a matter of protecting the company's investments. Such strategy placed ITT in an ideal situation to parlay World War II into an economic triumph. Behn was one of the few who could make meaningful long-range plans — no matter which side won. He waited, watching the fortunes of war, until a discernible pattern of victory emerged. Then, *shazam* — although ITT had been accused of Axis collaboration at the beginning of the war, Behn emerged as a conquering Allied hero, of sorts. He was the man with strong political influence and business interests all over Europe. As the Allied armies mopped up, Behn was personally on the scene to restore the ITT empire before the military governors could piece things together. And even more remarkably, ITT managed to carry off the role of victim of World War II and file a $30 million claim for damages which recently the United States government has seen fit to pay. So, with discreetly applied pressures and much chutzpah, Behn managed to have it both ways. If the Germans had won, who could tell what rewards would have befallen the faithful industrial empires of Krupp, Siemens, Mercedes, and the several German equivalents of ITT.

   ITT moved out of the worldwide conflict and into a period of predictable change in Europe and unpredictable confusion at home. Behn's adventures in the postwar TV and appliance business proved surprisingly disastrous. As losses mounted it became the considered opinion of a new ITT board of directors that Colonel Behn had outlived his usefulness. With Behn's grudging approval an ex-AT&T executive, General William Harrison, was elected as president and he and Behn continued the management of the company in an uneasy partnership. The relationship was hostile, their policies ineffective, and the company continued to founder.

Now the cold war was on. Problems in expanding the ITT international system were everywhere. But Behn was now violently anticommunist — American and European governments were in the same mood. As industrialist-patriot he managed to convince the European government agencies and the Federal Communications Commission in the United States to allow ITT more authority in the international telecommunications business. Submarine cables were laid; military communications links were built. Wherever he went, Behn taught his managers to play international politics and local politics and to maneuver to take advantage of the fears and alarms of the cold war. In a sense the first truly multinational corporation was being formed. Its home was now nowhere, its operations were everywhere, and responsibility for any subsidiary, division, or affiliate was hard to identify with a nationalistic or even geographic interest.

Finally in 1956 Colonel Behn ran down. Thirty-six years after he founded the company, he retired. In April of the same year, General Harrison died. Faced with an operating vacuum, the ITT board's personnel selection committee frantically combed the most secret files of the country's top executive recruiters. They pleaded with the "head hunters" to find a hard-nosed genius in the ITT mold, unhappy in his situation and ready to accept "the big challenge." The name offered by the most convincing recruiting firm, Boyden Associates, was Harold Sydney Geneen, then executive vice president of Raytheon. He was known as a financial executive who knew how to make profits happen. Geneen was tapped and he was interested. He studied ITT's record and potential. Profits were good, procedures sloppy, management diffused, and control poorly decentralized. Here was a chance to exercise every daydream Geneen had allowed himself, an opportunity most managers go to their graves never daring to wish for. A financially sound empire, worldwide, with possibilities unlimited and no one in charge. A lovely money-making machine all wound up and ready to respond to the right touch. Geneen's decision was easy; he left Raytheon to set up housekeeping in the dreary twelfth-floor offices of the ITT skyscraper in New York and began his reign. ITT management in particular, and the world in general, have never since been allowed to forget that this was the day the Messiah arrived.

Harold Sydney Geneen

WITH AN APPOINTMENT at the Pentagon canceled and nothing to do on a rainy afternoon in Washington, I decided to do a bit of research on my new employer. Settled comfortably in the main reading room of the Library of Congress, I began the magazine and newspaper gathering process, routine to the investigator's practice. After four hours I came away amazed at how little was published about ITT — and what had found its way to the printed page sounded suspiciously like the jargon of the company's public relations staff.

To be sure, there was extensive coverage of the successful and unsuccessful merger attempts, government pronouncements, newspaper editorials pro and con, *Fortune* profiles of the company's progress and *Wall Street Journal* news-and-views articles. But probably as the PR men intended, the ITT I knew did not come across.

However, distorted and stylized as it was, there was more substance to the picture of ITT than there was to the business profile of President Harold Geneen. Inside the company, Geneen is an omnipotent figure, carefully studied by a management who must be able to analyze both a business situation and also Geneen's reaction to it. The shadowy figure that appeared in the business literature lacked depth and perspective — it certainly was not the chief executive the ITT managers saw in daily confrontation.

To understand the implications of the economic and political power ITT holds, a working knowledge of Geneen and his system and style of management is necessary. What follows might be considered the essential Geneen, a combination of history, personal observations, and the comments of critics and supporters intimate enough with HSG to separate the fact from the folklore.

There seem to be several Geneens. First, the pre-ITT Geneen, a semi–Oliver Twist character who overcame an unhappy childhood to become a successful businessman, rising to executive vice-presidency of the Raytheon Company after a thirty-year career which had its ups and downs. Next, Geneen the ITT president, chairman of the board, and chief executive officer–dynamo of the world's largest multinational business, probably the most successful executive in the business world today. And finally there may be the retired Geneen in his post-ITT days. As a tease for business historians, he has indicated an interest in serving the government during this twilight period, when and if it ever comes. Washington and Wall Street beware.

Harold Sydney Geneen was born in England and brought to the United States by his parents as an infant. His father and mother were divorced and he spent his childhood in private schools and summer camps, his home life consisting of brief visits and occasional holiday vacations. At the age of sixteen he left school to live on his own in New York. He recalls the life of a page on the New York Stock Exchange as one of loneliness, poverty, and long, hard hours of work and study.

"I used to buy bread and taffy because it was inexpensive and filling. I'd go for weeks eating nothing else." A page from Franklin's *Autobiography*, at least.

He studied nights at New York University and finally in 1938 earned an accounting degree. He drifted out of the stock market, joined Librand, Ross Brothers, and Montgomery and began his financial apprenticeship in the large Manhattan accounting firm. In a successful if not spectacular way, he moved from company to company, up the ladder from accountant to comptroller to financial vice president. By the early fifties he had worked for American Can Company, the container makers; Bell & Howell, the camera people; and Jones & Laughlin, the steel giant — changing industries as readily as he changed companies. By reputation he was a tight-fisted, hard-driving executive with a track record of successful cost reduction programs.

That combination of qualities seemed to be exactly what Charles Francis Adams, chief executive officer of Boston's Raytheon Company, was looking for at the time. The Adams family, one of America's oldest in direct line from the early presidents, owned the electronics-oriented company and had successfully managed it with family members until the post–World War II period. But like many wartime prime contractors, Raytheon had overexpanded and placed too many of its eggs in the military systems and hardware basket. The company was having trouble recovering its peacetime status. A strong executive who could centralize authority and cut costs was needed, and that was certainly the way Harold Geneen's résumé read.

Predictably, Geneen began his Raytheon program with massive reforms. At first he was given complete authority, but as time passed, Boston conservatism seemed to require that Adams retain some control. Geneen and Adams argued continually about company policy and, although Adams assured Geneen that he had his confidence and a free hand, the audits and controls increased. Geneen chafed under such paternal authority. Finally, after a particularly stormy session in June 1959, Geneen cleaned out his desk and walked out the door with an ITT offer in his pocket. The stock market reflected Raytheon's problems and Geneen's frustrations by dropping Raytheon's stock six-and-a-half points the day he resigned.

"It was like driving a fast car at high speed and having someone occasionally tug at the wheel," Geneen later recalled. "When you can't solve your environment, change it."

Thus ended the pre-ITT Geneen experience. With a somewhat checkered career behind him at the age of forty-nine he was faced with the biggest challenge of his life. He had left Raytheon without solving the problems of the company's readjustment to peacetime economy to become president of ITT and face exactly the same problems. It took guts and confidence, but Geneen had never been short on either quality.

ITT confidence in its foreign operations had been badly shaken by World War II. After the war the company tried to establish a U.S. base but suffered severe losses from investment plunges in the volatile markets of television, consumer appliances, and industrial electronics. ITT management was conservative, diffused in authority, and had no central control. The New York headquarters was a "post office drop" and individual divisions were autonomous and managed by their presidents. The organization consisted of a loose confederation of fifty-three companies and divisions, most of them involved in telecommunications and electronics businesses. Each company guarded its technical secrets and markets against incursion by the others as jealously as they did by competitors. The ITT system was plagued by financial mismanagement, excessively high production costs and duplication of effort. Geneen himself could not have written a better scenario in anticipation of his arrival on the scene.

The coming of the financial Messiah was a rude shock to the complacent management of ITT. He began a program of cost reductions, personnel relocations, and, most disturbing of all, mass firings. At ITT he had the carte blanche he was never given at Raytheon, and he used it.

After the dust settled from his first months in office, Geneen realized that there was no blueprint for the future of ITT and the only way he knew to prosper was to expand, somehow. He began forging his master growth plans in the dark days of 1959 when ITT sales were less than a billion and the company's traditional markets were being seriously challenged both in the United States and abroad. But he

refused to accept limitations; his plans were bold, grandiose, and a rude shock to the few remaining conservatives
on the ITT board of directors. But he laid them out as all or
nothing proposals, and the Board voted to go along.

Geneen laid his career squarely on the line. After the
Raytheon imbroglio he had to field a winner or look forward to the long road down to middle management, which
would have by now yielded him a gold retirement watch
and a modest pension. He carefully assessed the problems
of foreign electronics acquisitions and the competition of
the two-company telecommunications club in the United
States from which ITT was excluded. American Telephone
& Telegraph Company and General Telephone Corporation were not inviting new members, and Geneen concluded that the danger signs were up in both directions. As
a consequence, he developed a business plan built around
moving ITT from its traditional markets into the service
industries, which he hoped would prosper from the predicted growth in population and gross national product.

Geneen was lucky. Because ITT stock was tied to a high
technology reputation, it performed much better in postwar markets than its earnings or financial statements war-
ranted. The stock market assigned high multiples to companies with concentrations in electronics, communications,
and defense. For better or worse, this was ITT's bailiwick.
The market gave Geneen his trading tender and he began
to assemble a staff of experts to advise him what and when
and how to buy.

Although his management style has changed over the
years, Geneen's personal philosophy remains much the
same as when he began the ITT adventure. He is the anti-

Renaissance man, unconcerned with the larger economic
and social issues of the times, immune to the frills and
trappings of his office, interested only in making ITT as
large, profitable, and dominating as possible within the
years his control spans. Now he is more blunt and direct,
more dictatorial and apt to command instead of persuade.
But he remains the master of basics; the philosophy he
expounds is that managers must manage. Hear the gospel
according to HSG.

On management style: "Well, I'm no laissez-faire, let-
me-know-how-things-are-in-six-months kind of guy. I want
to know what's going on. I don't want some proud guy to
get into his own Vietnam and suddenly hand me his resignation. Hell, his resignation couldn't bring back the ten
million dollars he'd lose."

On work: "Sure, a lot of guys bitch around here about
the long meetings, detailed reports, and hard work. But no
one complains anymore about the crazy decisions that
come out of New York headquarters."

On organization: "Around here, we run a colonial empire with 400,000 employees in sixty-seven countries; and
we're writing our own management book in the process."

On managers: "Personnel surgery is the only thing this
company needs on a continuing basis. You build discipline
in a company and the company will perpetuate itself.
Those who can't immerse themselves in their jobs just
won't make it at ITT. We want good, solid guys and the
magic word is interest. If he's interested, you can't get him
away from his work. After we've had a guy for a year, we
know what he's like."

On reports: "Being smart is only getting all the facts. My

guys have to find the genuine snapping turtle from the general turtle population. I want their reports to specifically, directly, and bluntly state the facts. Not high-flung rhetoric. Just facts. Reports that include action recommendations, a summary of the problems, reasons why the recommendations are being made and the specific position of the manager preparing the report. We allow no bull or evasion."

On monopoly: "If we are to compete overseas, we can't be hamstrung at home. We will resist any attempt to deprive us of our proper rights. It is clear that whatever the guise, by imaginary and legal means, what we are experiencing are direct attacks on bigness as such."

On executive suites: "My office is my briefcase."

Proving he is clairvoyant, on military business: "I'd rather have my money in South America. Chile, for example."

On government: "Our (————) government is about to run the country down the drain. Everyone in the government is really (————). They haven't the courage to tell the kids they can't have the ice cream and cookies three times a day. You've got to put some dignity back into business."

On his job: "My job is the most complex management job in the country. I've never met a man who could keep up with me."

On his company: "I won't be satisfied until this is the best damn company in the world."

On his troops: "Around here, management is the bailing wire that keeps everything in place. They don't quit, they don't strike, they just keep the place going. Those who can't immerse themselves completely in the job just won't make it here."

And finally, on Geneen: "If I had enough arms, legs, and time, I'd do it all myself."

Feel you know Harold Sydney Geneen a little better? He doesn't make many public statements; but when he does, it's certainly not high-flung rhetoric, generalities, or evasion. No one has ever criticized him for not telling it like it is, or at least as he thinks it is — except, of course, at congressional investigations. He does suffer lapses of memory on such occasions — but then, no one is perfect.

When Geneen began picking up the pieces at ITT in 1959, he used a lifelong study of General Motors as his model. GM's organizer, Alfred Sloan, was his personal hero; and the job of remaking ITT became a casting job in the General Motors' mold. Finance was made a direct reporting function throughout ITT, engineering responsibility was centralized, and a large technical staff began to grow into dominance. ITT managers made in-depth studies of the policies under which General Motors operated. "If it's good enough for General Motors, it's good enough for ITT," was the new anthem; and the Geneen-directed juggernaut began to roll on that high-octane formula.

Geneen's success in the beginning lay in his ability to shape the total environment in which ITT operated. All controls were centralized and he was the prime mover. Riding the crest of a stock market boom, he out-traded, out-bought, and soon out-distanced even "go-go" conglomerates like Litton and LTV. The companies ITT acquired were treated to the most liberal financial interpretation, sometimes to the consternation of the national accounting fraternity. He was accused of taking advantage of legal loopholes and fudging when necessary to optimize balance sheets and operating statements. He was charged with manipulating stocks and securities. And he was routinely accused of wooing politicians on all levels to support his running battle with the Justice Department whenever it sought to enforce the antitrust regulations vis-à-vis ITT. But, whatever his methods, the value of ITT stock increased and, as it did, his acquisition program accelerated.

Geneen's life style, as distinguished from his managerial style, is simplicity itself. After divorcing his first wife, he married his former Bell & Howell secretary. They acquired a home on Cape Cod, Massachusetts, and live in peaceful separation — he working, and she providing the pleasant setting in Manhattan and at the beach.

Geneen is a loner. Few people pretend to his friendship. From time to time he is persuaded to fish or play golf or watch a topless review; but mostly he works, sunup to long after sundown, seven days a week. As a cocktail party host he can come across as a quiet, introspective, chubby little man with a friendly smile, who insists you try the hors d'oeuvres because they cost a hell of a lot of money. In the heat of the General Managers' Meeting, he can be bitter, cynical, hypercritical — an abusive martinet, absolutely alone in the seat of power. One can only speculate on which is closer to the real Mr. Geneen.

Geneen's acquisition carnival has rolled on for years

without serious opposition from abroad. His simplistic approach to business outside the United States is ideally suited to tradition. Foreign politicians feel it is sufficient for the company to build a plant, support an election, or provide some other service to elicit a cooperative attitude in return. Monopoly is not a bad word, competitors establish cooperative relationships, and the intercession of the benevolent government against unions and the general rabble can usually be arranged.

This has not been so in the United States. Although Geneen invested heavily in public relations, propaganda, lobbying, and outright support of political campaigns, the effects were never wholly satisfactory. From the first Geneen found ITT business in the United States was more difficult to transact; congressional committees became increasingly hostile and suspicious, and the Justice Department began accumulating a large ITT file.

Finally the crunch came. Geneen had long been frustrated at being excluded from the telecommunications industry in the United States, prime area of the company's major technical expertise around the world. He tried several times to make incursions on the well-protected territory of American Telephone & Telegraph Company and the General Telephone Company, but the two giants had little trouble in brushing away the competition. Geneen did not buy the "AT&T at home, ITT abroad" formula any longer — but there seemed little he could do about it. ITT was forced to limit its activities to the acquisition of telecommunication component manufacturers, and attempting to build a communications satellite technology.

To flank the giants, Geneen completed in April 1966 negotiations to purchase the American Broadcasting Company. The Justice Department was somehow persuaded to approve the merger and, after some heated debate, the Federal Communications Commission also acceded in September 1966. ABC management was won over by promises of future rewards, and the widely-advertised shaky financial position of the company assured no negative stockholder reaction. ITT celebrated the founding of its United States communications empire.

But then, for the first time, the Congress stepped in. The Senate's Antitrust Subcommittee chastised the Justice Department and Federal Communications Commission for approving the merger. The Federal Communications Commission was accused of making mockery of public responsibility. ITT was required to allow congressional scrutiny of their records, and the government auditors were appalled at what they saw. Senators Wayne Morse and Philip Hart vehemently opposed the merger and were most vocal in their criticism of the FCC. Finally the Congress was able to place enough restrictive provisions on the merger to make Geneen withdraw.

This defeat drew the ITT battle lines with Congress, the Securities Exchange Commission, and the Justice Department. Geneen's acquisition blitzkrieg had been halted — temporarily. But the company prospered, quarter by quarter, with consecutive increases in income and per share earnings. And soon Geneen began again to make significant acquisitions, including the Hartford Insurance Company. Geneen was now willing that each major objective be won as the result of a congressional slugfest. No longer Mister Nice Guy, he took off the gloves after the ABC rebuff, and the Queensberry Rules were forgotten.

Geneen and the ITT he governs are enigmatic, representing themselves in different ways to different audiences. To the business community in the United States, Geneen represents order. Many businessmen yearn for the condoned monopoly, the controlled environment. Abroad the cartel system as it functioned before World War II is fondly remembered. To foreign entrepreneurs the Geneen style is the sensible way to run a business. And for ITT stockholders, he is the man who bootstrapped the company from $700 million to over $7 billion sales level in ten years, while chalking up over sixty consecutive quarterly increases in per share earnings. In Geneen parlance, these are all real unshakable facts for his critics to ponder.

Mr. Geneen is not the American Management Association's ideal manager in the approved pervasive style, nor probably anyone's favorite boss. He is accused of being impatient, brutal, arbitrary, and irreverent. His only discernible goals are grinding increases in revenues and profits for each and every quarter. For good or evil he is the model of a compulsive worker, organizer, and builder. And probably the world's most successful executive.

A *New Yorker* cartoon was thumbtacked on a bulletin board in the ITT Washington Office. With rising charts in the background, a caricature of a plump, balding business executive was addressing the annual stockholder's meeting. The caption read, "And though this year, as in previous years, your company has had to contend with spiraling labor costs, exorbitant interest rates and unconscionable government interference, management was able once more, through a combination of deceptive marketing practices, false advertising and price fixing, to show a profit which in all modesty, can only be called excessive."

Someone had carefully printed in blue ink in the margin, "HSG — our fearless leader."

The Washington Office

If the brains of ITT were in New York City in the late sixties, the heart of the company was in the nation's capital. The ITT Washington Office was staffed by a colorful lot of lobbyists, technical specialists, marketeers, consultants, and sales representatives, all living in a loose confederation of cliques and tribes. The ITT Building on L Street was the main area of activity. Adjacent to the Mayflower Hotel and strategically located in downtown Washington, it commanded the network of satellite offices scattered around the city.

With representatives from divisions in many industries and experts in a broad spectrum of technologies, the cumulative clout of the ITT Washington organization was awesome indeed. When all the forces cooperated and an objective was clearly identified, no task seemed beyond accomplishment. However, intercompany politics, feuds, divisional competition, and personal ambition were always in evidence. The effectiveness of the organization was far below what the money poured into its coffers should have commanded. There were simply too many people representing diverse and overlapping interests to achieve much harmony of purpose. Dog was always eating dog, or at least sharpening a fang or two.

The Washington Office proper and the entire capital show for ITT was run by William R. Merriam. Bill was the scion of an old Washington family, well connected enough socially to give ITT the aura of respectability it so badly needed in some circles. He was a public relations man with a pleasant, soft-sell personality — but, alas, a weak administrator. The support of President Geneen and the ITT super-chiefs in New York was the only way Merriam maintained discipline among the unruly ITT cohorts. After years of trying various organizational permutations and combinations, "good ol' Bill" finally gave up altogether. He fell back on ITT divisional management to keep their own people in line while he personally directed a few key lobbyists. The consequence was happy, freewheeling anarchy. When you worked with the Washington Office, you were more likely to be working with an individual than a team. No matter how sensitive the situation, tactics and strategy came not from the councils of Merriam and his advisors but from the lobbyists and marketing men in your field — and the legal consultants, of course. The fluidity of such a situation was often helpful, but it did have its disadvantages. While you were more or less unrestricted in getting the job done, you were at the mercy of Washington lobbyists like Dita Beard or Larry Farrell and their choice of contacts and acquaintances. Yours was the responsibility, theirs was the credit and prestige. Theirs was the tab and yours the responsibility of paying for it. This power vacuum existed partly because ITT top management did not want to be involved in the necessary but odious byplay which was the politicking way of life in the nation's capital.

The unlikely combination of Merriam and Dita Beard (then a secretary) organized the ITT Washington Office in the early 1960's out of a loose confederation of divisions. It grew from a "hang your hat while in town" office to a political powerhouse in ten short years. Bill and his charges danced everywhere about the capital while the great puppeteer Geneen directed activities from New York. The combination produced a formula for success in "big league" politics envied and admired by critics and the competition.

Legend has it that Merriam got his job through Kennedy aides who arranged for him to be in a receiving line with Harold Geneen at a White House reception. Properly briefed, President Kennedy introduced Merriam to Geneen as a good friend and a guy who really knew his way around Washington. Always impressed by the power of politics, Geneen returned to New York and announced to the board of directors that too little emphasis had been placed on Washington relations, and some quick changes were to be made by way of remedy. Merriam was hired and given a commission and budget to match.

The so-called "corporate people" were Merriam's Praetorian Guard. They reported only to him. Each was chosen for a special talent or skill and usually had connections with either the Democratic or Republican party. Most were sensitive political specialists who could be relied on like secret agents. They occupied the coziest offices, had the largest expense accounts, and were asked the fewest questions about their activities. In more humble circumstances in the organizational scheme were the marketing people and technical specialists. They represented divisions and subsidiaries that leased space from Grand Landlord Merriam. At the bottom of the social scale were a mysterious group of technical experts and liaison people who rotated in and out of the Washington Office on short tenure.

Typical of "corporate people" was the Lone Ranger and Tonto team of Tom Casey and Tom Gallagher. Casey was a tall, gray-haired, distinguished-looking Harvard Business School type — a Kennedy Boston import dubbed air force undersecretary. In the tradition of the bureaucracy, when administrations changed Casey joined ITT and stayed around to become a top-drawer military liaison man. Gradually he worked his way to the apex of the ITT military marketing corps and was considered the Pentagon's pipeline to Geneen, via Executive Vice President Rich Bennett. To compensate for his soft-sell, deferential style, Casey recruited a loud, uncouth ex-navy captain as his deputy. Tom Gallagher had spent most of his career as a navy flier and project manager — a desk-thumping, hard-drinking member of the "tail hooker" fraternity who headquartered at Washington's Aviation Club. He was one of a large number of military retirees who became "commercial representatives." They were an unusual lot. Although sales was their function, they were prevented by law from actively selling to the military for three years after discharge or retirement. But, being clever in the methods of Pentagon procurement, they found ways around such awkward regulations. Lunch and cocktail hours were used to maximum advantage, as were the golf course and private club. By and large, they performed their marketing chores without setting foot inside the Pentagon. Their techniques might be shabby and inept by professional standards, but they relied on personal equations to overcome the limitations of marketing finesse and product knowledge.

It was a lucrative game — for a while. The "representatives" exploited contacts and an intimate knowledge of certain military programs for as long as both lasted. The span was usually two to three years. Wild parties, magnificent expense accounts, weekends at game preserves and on the sea in yachts. Always lots and lots of money. Then, as had to happen, friends retired or were transferred and new program groups formed. The "representative" became ineffective and was gradually removed from the scene to be replaced by a more recent model. He had been milked of his useful information, and his contacts had lost their influence. Paradoxically, he was put out to pasture just at the time when he could have legally started to ply the selling trade.

Tom Gallagher was going through this metamorphosis. He was gray at the temples, bald and freckled on top of his bullet head, and wore the perpetual scowl of an old salt. His round, 300-pound form looked much like a bull elephant. He displayed the purpling gills of a professional good-time Charley and serious entertainer. But he was a man on the go. Day after day, with bumbling vigor, he carried out the duties of his office. ITT management found him effective as a confidant, messenger, and low-level influence broker. At times he drank his lunches and was difficult to handle, but he was loyal and never questioned an order. In short, a comfortable character, accepted by company managers and military buyers for what he was, a phenomenon of Pentagon procurement policies. Obviously a transient character in the business world, still he made military-contracts people feel safe, and even encouraged them to promote the award of a fat contract to ITT into a few special favors from the company's grab bag.

Casey, on the other hand, was smooth and cool, with all the moves of a master magician. In a few short years he had bamboozled the ITT top brass in New York into believing he controlled many key Democratic politicians. He also carved out for himself alone the responsibility for dealing with the most senior Pentagon brass. Geneen saw through Casey — but used him as he used the palace guards. Casey was a man who could be totally controlled and manipulated, had the ability to establish rapport with people in high places, and wanted to play for high stakes. A chap after Geneen's own heart.

Unfortunately for Casey, he had somehow angered Dita Beard. What the particular embarrassment had been no one seemed to know, but Dita had sworn a curse on Casey's head, and treated him to all the snares, delusions, and booby traps reserved for her worst enemies. Since both of them competed directly for Geneen's attention, Dita resented Casey's "Johnny-come-lately" claim to equal status.

Dita had scurried hard as a devout Republican during the Kennedy and Johnson administrations; she became irate at the insinuation that Casey, a Democrat, could pretend to her status with Nixon in the White House.

Tom and Dita were totally different in style. Dita was a graduate of the blood-and-guts school of getting things done in Washington. Tom was the sorcerer, a spinner of mysterious parapolitical webs. His multiple intrigues produced more frustration than Dita could easily endure and some of their weekly confrontations were O.K. Corral shoot-outs. But with New York's support Casey managed to hold his Pentagon position and keep Dita at bay — quite a trick, since facing Dita head-on meant contending with her political allies and their guerrilla tactics, from tax audits to tapped telephones.

To achieve a "grass roots" control ITT established a unique surveillance system for politicians. Every senator, congressman, governor, and important state official was assigned to a senior ITT manager for "cognizance" on a geographical basis. The manager was responsible for making the politician's acquaintance and being available on any occasion when he might require some service. A routine report was made by the ITT manager concerning the activities, disposition, and temper of his charge. The system was worked out by Senior Vice President Gerrity, to be sure that an ITT political "button man" could be activated on short notice whenever and wherever needed. Cumbersome, perhaps, but effective — and most ITT managers enjoyed their small political intelligence contribution to the great scheme.

The talents of a Tom Casey, Larry Farrell, or Dita Beard or any of the other corporate specialists were available to all of the company's senior marketeers — but on a priority basis. Competition for their time was keen. For Continental sales managers they pushed Twinkies for the armed forces cafeterias and for Defense Space Group vice presidents they convinced customs officials that ITT could detect fillings in the teeth of Mexican wetbacks. It was like selecting your own fourth-down-goal-to-go ball carrier. You had to decide which of the lobbyists had the most experience and expertise relating to your particular problem. Once selected, they took the ball and lit out for the goal line; and you blocked a bit where you could. If they didn't score, they lost some face; but chances were that your loss would be much greater — perhaps a large chunk of next year's sales, or even the benefits of employment.

The New York staff disliked the Washington corporate people, but admired them grudgingly.

"The bastards spend money like it was going out of style, but they deliver the goods," a staff controller said. "So when we bitch, we are told to cover it up and forget it."

A marketing specialist, sour-grapes style, allowed, "Sure they are good. But don't ever go down there with a lost cause or any project less than sensational; they only take on the big deals and the sure winners."

The legal staff in New York also disliked the corporate Washington representatives, but for a different reason than their accounting brethren. They saw the corporate playboys as a devil-may-care, Russian roulette–playing troupe who enjoyed getting tough with the military and civil service brass. The lawyers worried a lot about the results of the continual confrontations and casual espionage. But they failed to appreciate that the tightrope acts were not as dangerous as they appeared. Supported by the company's resources, the brinkmanship that went on was largely illusion. The ground was always well prepared in advance of any derring-do and major confrontations happened only when a favorable outcome was assured.

So, cuss them out and disparage their roles as we did, when the going got tough, ITT division managers ran to seek the advice of an ITT lobbyist — and usually the result was a ploy that worked.

On one occasion when my Cable Division marketeers had exhausted all strategies and were about to show a white feather in a contract dispute, I turned to one of Merriam's lieutenants for help. We had trooped the line, ensign through admiral, in an attempt to sell our system. But it soon became apparent that the web of Navy protection was being spun around the contracting officer and the award was about to be made to our competitor. Merriam blew the whistle, and an ITT lobbyist took a week to study our "case," then called us in for a consultation.

He was less than impressed with our efforts. "You're overmatched. No matter how technically effective you think you are, it is stupid trying to go this on your own. You need some muscle, and the sooner we bring it to bear, the better."

With our fate in the balance, he began the sideshow. Feet on the desk, he drew a yellow legal pad out of his drawer and began to doodle. He drew three lines on the paper and, as we watched patiently, he began filling the columns with names of senators, administration officials, congressmen, and one or two senior military officers.

"First list are the guys we own. Second list are the guys we can usually count on, people who owe us something. Third list are just influential guys, not friends but people who will negotiate for a deal."

He ticked off a dozen names, skipping from column to column. "These are the congressional types who will influence the procurement," he said. "Lucky for you boys we have some kind of major manufacturing facility in just about every one of their states."

He waved his pencil and continued the lecture. "When you work with these politicians, remember you have to prepare the whole goddamned smear. Write the letters, the "off the cuff" comments, the press releases, everything. Believe me, they use most of our stuff; some don't even proofread what we write for them. More often than not we arrange for releases. The responsibility we accept is to keep them out of trouble and to be sure that ITT is not embarrassed."

He paused for dramatic effect, looked out the window and studied a heap of rubble someday destined to be a subway terminal. Finally he said, "We can line up most of the guys you need and neutralize the ones that might come out against you. You really are lucky — we have one hell of a payroll in some of these states." He handed me the list. "Take this along and learn something about the legislators I've checked. I'll arrange some meetings in the next couple of weeks. Give Rich Bennett my regards when you get back to New York."

As the Eastern Airlines shuttle plane lurched through the sky from Washington to New York, I reread the list. With most of the people on the list pulling for us we could have arranged a war with Red China or an embargo on Japanese transistor radios. I wondered how it was possible to broker so much power so casually.

Dita Beard played her politics as a commercial enterprise. "These guys are businessmen, pure and simple. They are in the business of getting re-elected; and if you are ever in doubt as to how to deal with the bastards, keep that in mind. It is a very rare son-of-a-bitch here in Washington who is so entrenched that his re-election is not the first consideration in any goddam thing he does."

"Don't use amateurs," was an ITT Washington Office dictum. "Wait until a guy has been around long enough to know the tricks of the trade. The pros know how to get elected, how to stay elected, and how to get their bills paid in the process." So much for freshmen congressmen and newly-appointed department undersecretaries.

The weird personalities patrolling the beat for ITT in Washington were stashed in nooks and crannies of the Washington Office, out of the way of the normal traffic. "Eddie the Expediter" was such a geek. Eddie was an aging "marketeer" with a consumptive appearance and an irritating apologetic manner. But to ITT top management involved in Pentagon affairs, Eddie was a most valuable man to have around. His specialty was the covert acquisition of classified information. Eddie had built a career on his intelligence contacts in the military establishment. His reputation for acting as a double agent between ITT and the Pentagon had been passed on for several generations of senior officers. He represented the generosity of ITT. Eddie would pay handsomely for significant bits of information and would always protect his source.

His credits were impressive. He could come up with a Top Secret Defense Concept Paper, a sensitive memorandum, or unpublished budget projections almost on request. Eddie never obtained anything officially so there was no accountability — and he was most careful to dispose of all documents once the information was viewed by the requesting party. ITT, of course, took no official responsibility for Eddie or his activities. In the finest tradition of the espionage agent, he was alone.

The information relating to budgets, projects, and military planning that Eddie dealt in was absolutely essential to the ITT scheme of obtaining business. The future must be known. Geneen would not be surprised. So, never mind that Eddie was, in fact, a spy; he was a credit to the Washington Office, a hero first-class — an ITT patriot who would crawl all the way out on the national security limb, whenever and however requested.

Unfortunately for Hero Eddie, he never got used to the exposure. He had ulcers and was subject to nervous breakdowns on a two-year cycle. But he was always patched up and quickly put back on station. The company could not afford to take him in from the cold for very long.

Geneen had a penchant for such espionage activities. High on the list of Washington people for ITT executives to acquire socially were agents of the FBI, CIA, and the military groups in the intelligence community. The ITT board of directors and top management were liberally sprinkled with ex-government security people, ex-CIA chief John McCone being the most celebrated. Anyone who had held a position in military or government intelligence was an employment candidate. The presence of these people seemed to give Geneen a sense of security and fitted with his belief that business success relies heavily on a maximum of insider information — and no surprises.

One of our Defense Space Group straw bosses had begun his career as a clerk at the Federal Bureau of Investigation and had parlayed this association into a senior ITT position. He worked hard to maintain contacts with the FBI and CIA, and was careful to note on his expense account report how frequently he lunched with security officials. But he was not impressed by the results of the company's "spook" program.

"Geneen tries to influence our foreign business through the CIA. He prizes all the information they give him. But I suspect they water it down and a lot of it is pure bunk. He may feel like an insider but I don't think the CIA trusts him. As long as he lets them use the foreign telephone companies as bases, they will throw him a bone now and then; but nobody — not even Geneen — is going to con them for long."

When the Washington office screwed up, they screwed up on a magnificent scale. The famous Dita Beard memo and the million dollar offer to the CIA for Chilean intervention were typical examples. A case in point was the indiscretion made by a certain Washington lobbyist just pounding the pavement on his appointed rounds. One of the new breed of liaison men in the ITT organization, he was working the Democrat side of the street and performing a holding action during the party's political eclipse under the Nixon administration. He kept the Democratic majorities in the House and Senate completely aware of ITT's "sympathy" for their causes and managed to neutralize much of the anti-Geneen bias. He used a suave appearance to play the social game, and his incisive political mind to reason the next move of the antimonopoly forces. His star was certainly on the rise. But, as all busy businessmen do when they become overextended, he fell victim to his day-to-day routine. He was detected making an unbelievably gauche payoff to a congressman by simply laying out several hundred dollars in fresh bills on the desk of a surprised secretary. He asked that she deliver them to the boss, and bid her a pleasant weekend. Just a last bit of business on a busy day. But the press picked up the story and the young man's protests of innocence fell on deaf ears. A demotion followed, and threats of banishment to an ITT upholstered version of Siberia.

"It was unprofessional," said a senior member of the lobbyists' fraternity. "As the Mayor of Newark said when they were sentencing him for grand larceny, one simply can't let such things become a matter of course."

But, of course, they did. Lobbyists with weekly payments to deliver were used to passing money around without much thought of the consequences of their actions — just as an espionage officer probably regards political murder in the same class with the audit of a saboteur's expense account. All in a day's work.

Few people in the Washington Office ever saw all of the ITT picture; most were aware only of the tip of the iceberg. Company involvements were too numerous to easily catalog. ITT negotiators constantly shuttled between New York and Washington to deal with the Justice Department, Security Exchange Commission or Federal Communications Commission. Company emissaries seemed always to be holding discussions with regulatory agencies at the highest levels. Comings and goings of these executives were kept secret, sometimes from members of their own staffs. Summaries of their activities were encrypted in CRYPTEL, the ITT company code, and transmitted daily to New York and Brussels. Unfortunately for military security, a considerable amount of classified information was transmitted through these networks as well, and some probably leaked out. ITT Washington representatives and the company top brass never seemed to feel that they had audit responsibility for such information, since it was given to them so freely.

Much of the confidential reporting to ITT New York management by the Washington Office was a marzipan-coated version of the real action. For the ITT board of directors the hard facts of survival and achievement in the political jungle were always glossed over. Board room conversation might be sprinkled with innuendos suggesting great political secrets and subversions, but the gentlemen were seldom exposed to the facts of the sabotage of a military career or the manipulation of a promotion for a senior civil servant. It was felt that board members and some ITT top management had not stomach for such bloodletting. And those that shared the hard-eyed philosophy of

the shock troops in the political battlefield preferred to
ignore the details.

Gradually over the years the Washington Office became
an entity responsible primarily to itself. These professionals
kept only a few people completely informed. They realized
that only success counted, the "go no-go" of obtaining contracts and arranging appointments, guiding legislation and
securing patronage — only specifics. If they performed
well, they survived; if they failed, they were cashiered.
And there were few questions asked as to how they had
achieved the objectives.

Backed by the company's carte blanche, the ITT Washington lobbyists became some of the most formidable
hucksters in the capital during the sixties and early seventies. With more and more cold cash poured into the quest
for favorable antitrust solutions to the company's problems, the senior lobbyists worked at creating their own
spheres of influence and a powerful base of support for
Geneen's acquisition plans.

Mendel's Party

ITT Propaganda Minister Ned Gerrity's organizational skill and Machiavellian abilities were displayed through his choice of Washington lobbyists, the most important "button men" of the public relations trade. They were a dedicated, effective and easily expendable crew, loyal lightweights who responded immediately to the Minister's stimulus. Larry Farrell was a member of this select group. He was a middle-aged, medium-sized Irishman in a traditional Celtic mold; a twenty-year veteran of the company's public relations and advertising staffs.

As a Gerrity prize pupil, Larry was selected for a senior congressional placement. He was assigned to Congressman Mendel Rivers, a liaison equal in importance to the Dita Beard shackle to Congressman Bob Wilson and the ties others in ITT had with Attorney Generals and FCC Commissioners. Such relationships represented the ideal public relations situation — an ITT agent at the courts of the mighty, a minister plenipotentiary to the powers in the Congress and Administration.

Congressman Rivers, as Chairman of the Armed Services

Committee, was probably the most powerful man in Washington after the President. A Southern legend in his own time — a Gumville, South Carolina, boy who survived a dirt-poor boyhood to rise to the foremost seat of power in the Congress. The man who controlled the fortunes of the Pentagon. The titles of Mr. Confederacy, Mr. South Carolina, Mr. Conservative suited him well — but his most important moniker was Mr. Moneybags to the military-industrial complex. A man of great potential worth to ITT.

Courtesy of Farrell, we were signed up for special seats at an elaborate congressional dinner honoring famous good gray Democrats. The $100-a-plate affair was a guaranteed sellout of the mammoth Hotel Sonesta ballroom. Our seats had been hawked by Congressman Mendel Rivers.

The mood was jubilant. The Democrats at that time were not admitting that Nixon was unbeatable in 1972 or that his image would improve in the time left until election.

"It's either Hube the Cube or Eddie Muskie," a Congressman confided. He pumped Rivers' hand and introduced an obviously affluent lady attired in ante-bellum style. "You know our state committeewoman, Mendel?" The jeweled lady curtsied, and Mendel brought her up like a bishop in a ring-kissing ceremony.

"Marvelous to meet you again. Just marvelous. Hope you're enjoying our little party." The charm of the southern professional politician was a good show indeed.

Farrell and I flanked Congressman Rivers, impressed by the ease with which he handled the party guests, as though it was his personal receiving line. He reminded me of a gifted undertaker who had learned to make the awkward matter of death an acceptable social ceremony in which he was the key figure.

When a portly, well-dressed gentleman showed in the line, Rivers turned over the reception duties to an assistant. Arm in arm, he led the newcomer over to where we stood.

"These gentlemen are from ITT, Horace," he said. "They are down here to pay a short visit, and I'd like for them to talk to you a little bit about some property they may be interested in down your way. Thinking about putting up some kind of a factory, you know."

Horace, of course, had been briefed and was duly impressed. After a few minutes of bland conversation, Farrell arranged to have him spirited away for more confidential chats with some senior ITT staff people. So, the problem of tax treatment for a large ITT investment was in the first stage of solution.

Rivers returned to the receiving line and shook hands warmly with a passing senator well known for his liberal stance. As the senator hurried away, Rivers growled, "That bastard doesn't see this country the way we do. He's not our kind of people, Larry." Farrell, the good disciple, nodded gravely.

"I can't understand those people, I really can't. What are they going to get out of passing this country out piecemeal?" Rivers shook his white head slowly. "But, hell, we had a good Democratic party before all this business started, and we'll have a good Democratic party after it's all past."

As a touch of Farrell's magic, any ITT manager without his lady was seated next to a sweet young thing, attractive lady, or interesting matron — whatever was appropriate. Producing such companionship was Farrell's stock-in-trade, of course, but still it was impressive. The lovely ladies were all introduced as wives of good Democrats who could not make it to the party, secretaries to Congressmen, or important senators' girls Friday: a charming and talented group, all of them with some small obligation to Larry, Congressman Rivers, or ITT, taking this delightful way to square things up.

"Who do you work for?" the blonde next to me asked. She was a quiet knockout in a black dress that pinched in at all the right places. A short skirt showed off perfect legs, and a ringlet hair-do placed her, I thought, between eighteen and twenty-five.

"ITT," I said.

"Oh, of course," she said, "I know you're a friend of Larry's and everyone at these tables is from ITT, in one way or another. I mean what group?"

No names, please.

"I'm with one of the electronic groups in California," I said, "just stopping over."

"And a good Democrat," she laughed. "ITT seems to be full of good Democrats on nights like these."

"Of course," I said. "ITT is divided into three parts — just like Gaul — good Democrats, good Republicans, and good Independents."

"Depending on whose party it is," she said. "Pardon the pun."

"We put in whatever team is most appropriate; but you must know that."

She shook her head, "No, I know very little about the company. I work for a Republican senator who sends me to these things as a spy. But I always have a good time. Choice duty, sort of."

In the course of the speeches and harangues that followed, she doodled Charlie Brown characters on the napkin.

"You ought to do the funnies," I whispered.

"There's enough material here for a year of comic strips," she said. "Every once in a while I get the urge. Herblock can't last forever."

At the intermission, we pushed out to the lobby and settled with a crowd of semi-tight Democrats in a small cocktail room. Over Manhattans, she began a familiar but engaging tale of her husband's long absence in Vietnam. She told the story with an impressive sincerity and little touches of humor and pathos. Blue eyes snapping, lashes fluttering, positioned seductively in the low light of the lounge — a proposition in the classic Washington style, but with much more charm than I'd seen since I dated at Miss Morningstar's Finishing School.

Caught up in the role of nodding and sipping, I encouraged the conversation along. These situations were amusing, flattering to the male ego, and easily controlled. Suddenly, I was clapped hard on the shoulder and heard an unpleasant twang over the cocktail lounge din.

"Got a minute?" It was Larry Farrell, sober and smiling. "Something important just came up. Will you excuse us, please? I'll order a round."

We walked out of the lounge to the lobby.

"You are about to disappear," he said.

"You can't be serious," I said.

He looked around the lobby and smiled to passers-by as he spoke.

"I think you and I can do business in this company. And so I think I'll keep you relatively uncompromised. Your table mate, proposing to be your bed mate, is a plant — I do believe. Something to generate one more entry into your personnel record. Not good, not bad; but the fewer entries on that side of the ledger, the better for you."

"I can't believe you're serious. Why the hell the high intrigue?"

"I don't know. Perhaps because you're new. Perhaps because someone wants to know something. Take my advice and go back and play a little knees and fingers, and then invent something to get out of the party. I'll take the check, and it's all over."

"Is she really a phony? I mean, she doesn't come across as the Dragon Lady."

"No, I don't think so. She's just about what she says she is. She does work for a John Birch senator, and her husband is over getting his ass shot off by some gooks. And she does enjoy the party scene; and she is, from time to time, in a mood to help people out, so to speak."

"I don't know why you're doing this, but I guess I should be grateful."

"Don't mention it," he said. "I'm doing it for a pound of flesh — some time in the future. And don't think I'm trying to rip her off for myself. You'll see me somewhere else later on — conspicuously alone."

"It's nice to know that there is an ulterior motive," I said.

"It's just that I think, if you're going to be playing a big game in Washington for keeps, you ought to stay somewhat snow-white. At least as far as our troops are concerned. It may help me, too."

The Democrats were still filing out when we got back to the table. Larry began a wild story about one of his Irish relatives in Brooklyn, in the midst of which he waved to the table a balding, paunchy navy captain.

"Are you going to the admiral's party?" the blonde asked. "I understand all of the ITT people will be there. And everyone is going over to Ryan's house later on. And who knows where from there?"

She was flashing a stunning smile. The captain was concentrated on drinking seriously. Another Farrell wave and we were joined by an ITT marketing vice president from Fort Wayne.

Farrell had to be straight, I thought. No other reason. Make it short and sweet. I stood. "Delightful to meet you," I said. "I do have an appointment with an old Academy buddy across town. Last chance to see him before he goes overseas. I'll look forward to seeing you when I drop in on the senator."

She looked surprised, but only for a second. The captain stumbled to his feet, and the Fort Wayne visitor was mildly confused. She smiled sweetly, "I'm really sorry. But call me at the office. I'm sure the senator would enjoy meeting you again."

I was stopped at the door by a bald, fat Democrat in a stylish ruffled tuxedo. "We'll bury the bastards in '72, right?" he said. As he pumped my hand I glanced back to see the blonde whispering to the Fort Wayne vice president. An alternate target had been established.

Larry never did collect his marker with me. A few months later Mendel Rivers died and Larry was reassigned to more prosaic marketing duties.

He reluctantly returned to the world of day-by-day journeyman lobbying and selling duties.

"I wonder if I can get back into the swing of escorting these marketing directors and hotshot division presidents." Larry said. We were having cocktails at the 21 restaurant in New York, scene of many of Larry's past adventures. "Do they still come down to Washington to win the billion dollar contract and spend an evening with someone that resembles Raquel Welch?"

"Sometimes they get the sequence mixed up," I said.

"I'll never hack it," Larry said. "I think I've played out my option. And even if I could resume that action, there are too many people with scores to settle to let me. The Rivers and Farrell partnership broke up too soon for Farrell, unfortunately."

Larry lasted only a few months after Rivers' funeral. A chain of extraordinary, if predictable, circumstances put him in conflict with first his Washington enemies, then the ITT New York Gestapo lieutenants and finally, Senior Vice President Gerrity personally. At the height of Farrell's counterattack, in a sure message from the Fates, he was hit by a golf ball while entertaining at an Acapulco convention for aerospace executives. Out of action for six weeks, lying in a Washington hospital, Larry was helpless and the opposition adroitly mopped up. When he came back to duty, there was very little left of his authority or responsibility. An expert at reading handwriting on ITT walls, Larry made quick checks of what support was available from old friends in high places. There was none. So with the politician's sense of the possible he negotiated a handsome settlement in exchange for his "retirement" after twenty years of loyal service.

He was sorely missed at the Crazy Horse Bar during the next Paris Air Show and important members of the aerospace and lobbying fraternities vowed to even Farrell's score with ITT at first opportunity. But Larry had taken a job as a consultant for a syndicate of scrap munitions dealers, operating out of Saigon. He prospered, forgave ITT and hardly missed Paris at all. Mendel Rivers would have been proud of him.

World Headquarters

ITT WORLD HEADQUARTERS was located on a grim, color-less, foreboding expanse of New York City known as Park Avenue. The ITT Building was across from a brightly colored church and up the street from a number of high-priced, second-rate hotels. The World Headquarters comprised two skyscrapers: the ITT Building on Park Avenue, and the North America's Building directly behind on Madison Avenue. The shuttle between the two buildings across a traffic-choked street was akin to the march between adjoining ant hills.

Most of the ITT offices were small and cramped. Stand-ard executive trappings consisted of a chrome and wood desk, a side chair, and a few company-furnished reproduc-tions on the walls. The manager added the inevitable pic-ture of the wife and kiddies at play. Concerned by bomb threats the ITT security guards randomly locked every second or third door, confusing traffic patterns and making each floor something of a maze. The secretaries held keys to the rest rooms, making it necessary for visitors to "sign up" with the girls to use the facilities.

"The old explosive on the flush handle rig is the one we are most concerned about," an ITT security guard said. "We can't account for every nut that walks into this building, so we have to take these precautions."

As one passed from floor to floor, the comings and goings of executive teams and management groups became obvious. When a group or staff was reduced or de-hired, rows of offices and secretarial desks were left empty — like a no man's land with the battle shifted to another front.

Even for the senior executives there was little attempt to create a pleasant mood or provide any relief from the task at hand. At the corner of each floor was an executive suite occupied by a vice president or senior staff executive. These offices were larger than the standard, but far less palatial than the officer's rank would warrant in most corporations. For the resident New York executive this was an unfortunate home away from home. But for the divisional and group executives maintaining token offices in New York and headquarters elsewhere, the austerity didn't matter since their suites at the factory were palatial.

Frank Deighan, my compatriot Division Vice President, was conducting me on an ad hoc tour of the headquarters complex.

"You'll be impressed by the Business Plan Arena. It's the gallows humor of American business."

We identified ourselves with the ITT security guards at a check point station by the entrance. They eyed my visitor's badge with suspicion but let us pass. The Business Plan

Meeting Room was large, long, and high, with fifty-foot tables on each side. Four projection screens hung high up on the walls. A spaghetti of wires from communication devices ran across the center floor and along the walls in all directions. The two tables described a gradual parabola on both sides of the room with thirty leather high-back chairs propped behind each one. The center between them was clear, arena style, except for four symmetrically-placed projectionists' seats.

"No smoking, soda water on the tables, and everyone with his own hand-lettered nameplate," Deighan said. "Slip it in when you come in. It's a funny sight to see some of these senior executives standing in the wings, waiting to come on with their goddam nameplates clutched under their arms. Like kids in a Christmas play . . . 'I am a Wise Man from the East' . . ."

"This is the place where Geneen holds forth every month?" I had heard tales of these continuing sagas.

"The same," Deighan said. "A hallowed ITT spot. More blue blood has been spilled around here, and more careers ended, than any one spot in American business." He pointed at the table on the right. "Geneen sits at the table center, facing the poor bastards on the other side of the room who are making their pitch. The General Managers Meetings are staged a little differently."

"Flanked by his hierarchy in regal rows, apparently," I said.

"Like a goddam chess lineup," he said, "the generalissimo and all his field marshals. And the son-of-a-bitch turns the temperature down until you're sitting on your hands."

"Geneen?"

"Goddam right. No dozing with him around. And when he takes it into his head to hold a little personal recess, everyone just sits and waits. All sixty or eighty people — with a goddam payroll that would build a couple of medium bombers. They just sit and make small talk and congeal and wait for the side meeting to end and HSG to return."

It was easy to imagine the lions-and-Christians episodes that went on during General Managers' Meetings and Business Plan Reviews. The Geneen system was based on such confrontations — meetings, oral reports, reviews, and more meetings. Geneen demanded to face the authors of the ITT business plans eyeball to eyeball. He took as much from how they performed as from what they said.

We arrived early at the ITT executive dining room and took a table by the window. The food was terrible but the service outstanding, and the view of the skyscraper canyons impressive. At each table was a stock market report, and the menus noted the calorie count next to each food listed.

"There are experts at table hopping here." Deighan waved around. "A technique for cornering people at lunch, which some guys have reduced to a science. I admire the kind of bastard who can make a political game out of any situation. Don't you?"

We were joined by a vice president, a General Electric retread who was Geneen's prime contact with the telecommunications industry around the world. At his elbow was one of his lieutenants, a product line manager for the wire and cable manufacturing facilities. Both were faint-

hearted supporters of the San Diego cable plant program.
The conversation was guarded and dull.

"The security thing bothers me," the vice president said.
"You are screwing around with some military secrets that
are probably better left untouched."

"Like what?" Deighan asked.

"Like the navy's antisubmarine warfare programs. Normally we don't clear anyone from Europe on these things.
The military boys are looking over everybody's shoulder
in that field — even the British are suspect. ITT doesn't
have a big stake in that kind of military business, so why
the hell get involved and take a chance on losing something
a lot more lucrative?"

"Geneen is queer for cable," the product line manager
said. "The son-of-a-bitch will put money into cable plants
when he won't invest in anything else. But cable certainly
isn't a gilt-edged security right now."

"When everybody else is getting manipulated, the cable
people get the investment. So why sweat the program,"
Deighan said. "Cable has always been easy to control in
other countries. Maybe we can do the same thing here."

The vice president shook his head. "Cable is like telephone systems and some other manufacturing franchises
abroad. You build a cable plant and the *presidente* or *general supremo* says that you will get the business. And you
don't have to be concerned about competitors growing up.
For some reason your able management doesn't seem to be
able to make the transition from what happens in Europe
and South America to what happens in the United States.
We are not leading the telecommunications pack here.

There is no chance for easy cable monopoly, and the investment risks are very high."

"So, why not tell Geneen?" Deighan said. "Just stand up at the next G.M.M. and say, 'Mr. Geneen, you don't know what the hell you're talking about.' Just like that. The guy has a sense of humor, I'm told."

The vice president looked wry and shook his finger at us. "You're fooling with something big. You would be amazed at the amount of official and casual espionage that goes on in this company. Some of the divisions are goddam close to using spook talk in their sales pitches. They sell to the Arabs one week and the Israelis the next, and the Indians the next and the Pakistanis the week after. You can't push military systems and hardware around the world and not expect to have little leaks here and there. In aerospace and electronics, it doesn't seem to be devastating; but I expect that if you compromise any antisubmarine warfare programs, you're going to put a lot of our people out of work."

Deighan shook his head and shrugged. "I'll pass the word."

The vice president turned and noticed a group entering.

"Pardon me," he said, "I've really got to catch Maurie for a few minutes." He left, luncheon entrée untouched.

"That's how it's done," said Deighan. "He is a master of the bump and run. Watch him work over the Defense Space Group crew."

Deighan turned to the product line manager, who was wolfing down a sandwich. "Not so fast, Dennis. What message do you bring us as our guide and counsel?"

The P.L.M. smiled crookedly and gulped, "The message

is that the barbarians are at the gate, buddy. You had
better start building pretty quickly on that salt marsh in
San Diego or your Silver Strand plot may all just fade
away."

"Just Before the Battle, Dita..."

JOHN RYAN WAS Merriam's deputy, a sharp, sincere guy, and not very happy about being given the assignment of neutralizing Deputy Attorney General Kleindienst. But, like everyone else, he did what he was told.

Gerrity's propagandists were in town, putting the finishing touches on a massive campaign to enlist congressional support. The stage was set for the big push. All available ITT managers were called on to man the Washington trenches, from legal vice presidents to satellite marketeers. The New York command post was ready to swing into action and the Brussels and Tokyo nerve centers would enlist foreign support.

Dita Beard said the whole antitrust thing was settled, and that the "goddam stupid New York bastards" were just trying to get into the act. But if it was overkill, as Dita insisted, it was worth the extra effort. The ITT executives whose jobs were on the line were leaving no margin for error. The Justice Department suit had to be settled and

ITT had to keep the Hartford Insurance Company. Geneen had issued the order: at any cost, we keep Hartford. No one knew who was going to be hurt in the process, McLaren or Kleindienst or Mitchell or the President himself. But the company was fighting for its life and somehow, some way, ITT would survive, no matter who had to be wasted along the way.

"Believe it or not," Tom Casey said, "Dita sponsored her first anti-Nixon luncheon for Republicans last week, just in case. Measuring the 'hate Ehrlichman' attitude, I suppose. But who needs all that? The company has manufacturing operations in forty states. Mobilize the locals, I told Gerrity. You've got a goddam grass roots movement, first class."

Whatever the grand strategy or tactical employments, it was apparent Geneen's army was readying to do battle. The forces of justice would never know what hit them.

The Staff System

WITH THE EMERGENCE of the business conglomerate in America in the early sixties came the re-emergence of centralized authority and the supervisory staff system of management.

President Ralph Cordiner's decentralized management system, as researched and perfected by the General Electric Company, was in vogue in the fifties — cheered on by management consultants and business school deans. The staff system robbed management of its entrepreneurial prerogatives, they said. It might be satisfactory for slow, cumbersome military-type organizations, but was unwieldy and unresponsive in the dynamic arenas of business. All of the negative adjectives were applied to centralized management. Professor Peter Drucker was hailed as the apostle of the new decentralized, line-oriented philosophy and the rush was on to reduce staffs to lean operating crews of specialists. Staff people of any stripe or skill were suspect.

Then along came the conglomerate — a management organization that operated like a central bank for both funds and talent. As the conglomerates gobbled up company after company and grew ever more profitable, opinions changed with respect to their management policies. Conglomerates assembled large, knowledgeable staffs to audit and control the acquisitions in many diverse business activities. Companies that thought they had reached a happy medium began to doubt their staff-line relationships. As the conglomerates surged ahead the desire to look like Litton or LTV or ITT was great enough to start the pendulum swinging. Gradually the circles of power became heavy with staff specialists, and the centralization of business management was back.

In understanding the *Darkness at Noon* atmosphere of ITT, it is necessary to understand how the staffs influenced policy. They operated like a cross between the secret police and a kindly family doctor. To a degree the staff was supreme so long as it reported all of the facts. But it also was required to confess when it was technically incompetent for a particular assignment. So staff people apologized a lot and mitigated their advice. But top ITT management knew that there was no way to run the company on the Geneen formula without heavy emphasis on the staff role.

ITT gradually developed a unique, efficient centralized operating system of line-staff management, both in organization and methods. In procedure it grew closer to the military general staff concept than that of any other major company, even to sporting an espionage organization and worldwide intelligence-gathering networks.

Unfortunately for Geneen's dreams and magnificent obsessions, ITT could never enjoy the leverage of General Motors or Dupont. It did not have the ability to dominate one or more major industries. The company seems destined to continue its piecemeal acquisition policies in diversified industries, ganging sales and profits to purchase the growth Geneen so dearly prizes. And with unrelated businesses in the assembly process at all times management control problems become ever more complex, resulting in a tendency toward increased centralization and larger and more specialized staffs.

The ITT staffs were peppered with graduates of the management consulting profession, people who could appreciate the manipulation of power as almost an academic exercise. They seemed to have no psychic need for profit and loss responsibility and were the stuff great audit groups are made from. ITT claimed to run the largest and most efficient management consulting company in the world, and continually proselytized some of the best talent away from the old-line management consulting houses to the consternation of their ultraconservative proprietors.

"The only difference between a management consultant and an ITT staff man," a senior vice president said, "is that if you don't accept the consultant's advice, he simply collects his money and leaves. If you don't accept the staff's advice, you leave." Another staff man said, "We get these M.B.A.'s from the Ivy League business schools all the time. But unless they learn our system, they don't last. We are taking the place of the Harvard Business School, so far as Geneen is concerned. He is proud of his Harvard tie, he lists the Business School Advanced Management Program

in his biography, but he balks at sending anyone back to
the program. He believes that we are the trail blazers, and
the rest of the business world is 'sucking hind tit.' "

The staffs had taken over some functions to the point of
completely emasculating division management. Financial
management and long-range planning were securely in
staff hands. They also controlled the operations research,
project management, and the market research and analysis which resulted in most of the company's acquisitions. Obviously, the staff chieftains reported directly to
Geneen.

"To get to the top in this company you've got to go
through one of the staffs," Frank Deighan said. He was a
graduate of Booz, Allen & Hamilton Management Consultants and seasoned by two tours with ITT staff groups.
"You may be operating well in the field, but it will only
be a matter of time before they want you back in New
York. If you're going to work on the top levels, the brass
must be sure of your reactions, gut and otherwise. You've
got to be able to hang tough — they have to be sure. In
short, you must become a known quantity. I thought the
guys at Booz were ruthless until I joined HSG and Company. But Booz guys were little old ladies with bleeding
hearts compared to ITT guys I've operated with."

As was intended, the staffs struck fear into the hearts of
the line management. There was a staff man always looking over your shoulder, and he was outside your jurisdiction and the control of your operating management. In
fact, sometimes the staff man was outside of any authority
or jurisdiction except the Office of the President. The staff

men were routinely rotated in assignments to avoid any rapport being achieved between division management and the staff. They were the Ogres of Operations, and headquarters intended to keep them that way.

The staff titles changed with the vogues of management policy. A fashionable one in the early seventies was "product line manager." To read the Product Line Manager's job description you would assume he was a combination general manager, marketing manager and financial specialist, all rolled into one. And functionally his assignment was impressive, including a number of companies, usually scattered worldwide, assembled by industry or product line. But in fact the P.L.M.'s were spies, pure and simple. Their responsibility was to carry back to the top management, and particularly Geneen, information concerning division operations. As with political commissars in Russian infantry regiments, their first function was that of informer, and their popularity was assessed accordingly.

The failing of these staff courtesans was often a superiority complex which allowed the line operators of the business to build up subtle defenses. Since the staff man could not know all of the key factors in the operation of the business he was always vulnerable to a technological sandbag or conflicting expert opinion. Only if he reached some kind of peace with his line counterpart would he be fed "straight dope" insofar as the real problems were concerned. So often there developed an Alphonse and Gaston relationship not unlike the deals made between top management and labor leaders. When some controversy was inevitable, the scene was rehearsed by staff and line secretly, before it got to the forum of a business plan or top management review. It was amusing to sit through such meetings knowing that even the friction and dissent had been contrived.

On occasion, the line and staff did battle without quarter. With so many people on both sides possessing a strong instinct for the jugular, such confrontations were usually mean, ugly, and counterproductive. But stimulated by top management interrogation, the staff had to make an occasional example of some errant or cocky division president.

"You watch your boss on the staff side and you get the signal," a North American staff manufacturing specialist said. "If Geneen and Bennett start zeroing in on some guy, you had better be able to pull out the sheet of embarrassing questions from your little black notebook and join in. *Au contraire*, if HSG is smiling, philosophizing, and telling stories about his old days in this or that industry, then we just clam up. No matter what we have on the division boss we make some obvious comment concerning how brilliantly the division is being operated and suggest, sotto voce, some minor changes. This is a totalitarian government, buddy, and we don't ever forget it. I've seen a few staff guys really go in and try to straighten something out in a division. Usually what happens is they start bailing water with the division management, instead of standing back and reporting how and why the ship is sinking. In a very short time, it affects the staff man's continuity of employment. New York doesn't want some guy in there trying to solve the problem. What they want is someone telling them who or what or where the problem is."

Criteria for selecting ITT staff men indicated, by nuance, the type of man that best fitted the role.

"Does he make recommendations based on a visibility of the situation not yet recognized by division management?"

"Does he keep cool, even during periods of violent disagreement with line managers?"

The requirements ranged from technical grasp to social presence, but came across as being much the same as those the CIA uses to select an agent.

The system of a staff man overseeing each major line function did not encourage an entrepreneurial business climate. But the staffs did provide direction, and could marshal a number of diverse technical skills very quickly to solve a problem.

Geneen's concept of forcing the divisions to constantly run their businesses "on paper" was policed by the staffs. Reports submitted by each division monthly were examined in detail by the assigned staff man. A system of marginal notations was developed by the staffs which allowed top management to analyze the problems, opportunities, danger signals, and errors contained in the reports after only a cursory glance through the thick notebooks. More than a few "red flags" meant heavy going for the division managers involved.

The disadvantage, of course, was that such Star-Chamber procedures often eliminated the opportunity for line people to explain their business. It was a temptation for a line manager to accept the recommendations of the staff with mild reservations, even though he might feel strongly that they were in error. By carrying out the recommendations to illogical conclusions and requesting further staff direction as the losses mounted, the situation might become embarrassing enough to drive off the staff men and allow the manager to reap the rewards of setting things right again. But the wise division chief took a mid-course. He rolled with the staff's punches and avoided any "knock 'em down, drag 'em out" arguments. On the other hand he made sure that his opinions were visible all the way up to Geneen. There were line operating heroes in the game, but not many persevered very long. Occasionally a recalcitrant division manager with a hot hand and a mushrooming business would batter the staffs for a while and run the spies off his reservation. But a dip in sales or an industry slowdown would come, and the staff would load up for the Business Plan Review. After a blood bath the manager was usually convinced that the cards were stacked against him; and he was a more docile candidate for advice in the future.

"I gained a hell of a lot more respect for the staff after they fried us at the Business Plan," a general manager said. "Mind you, not respect for their ability. I don't think some of them know their ass from a hole in the ground. But let me tell you, they know how to play the game. They sat on the other side of the table with all the questions, while my managers sat over here and tried to come up with answers, poor bastards. I'm not fool enough to put us in that situation again, let me tell you!" After a session or two of such guerrilla staff action, the general manager doesn't intentionally antagonize the apparently timid, self-effacing staff man who drops in at division headquarters and apologetically asks a few simple questions.

All ITT staffs, of course, operate most effectively within the spheres of proper activity that Geneen defines. Their stock in trade is an insight into the operational activities they monitor. They can't be omnipotent so they will concentrate in the areas where they feel Geneen's prime interest lies. The worst disaster is to bone up technically in a particular field and then learn that Geneen's interest has strayed elsewhere. So, even Geneen's key staff people often seem on thin ice. They apologize quickly, recant often, play the humble role to perfection — and probably pray a lot that the Messiah will guide them. But they remain: the continuity of the staff man at ITT is much longer than his line brother. They have the permanence of court jesters and hunt masters who watch the captains and prime ministers come and go.

The staffs are constantly reorganizing; but generally they are made up of controllers, corporate development people, lawyers, tax experts, real estate consultants, and the like — usually between fifteen and twenty disciplines. Staff men like to stay in their particular field and are very quick to recommend outside consultants and specialists when they encounter unusual problems. They enjoy spending money for advice — passing along with it the responsibility for failure.

Geneen regards himself as a pioneer in the centralized management techniques of the computer age and his formulas work very well for him. What will happen when the great man is no longer around to exercise complete autonomy is a matter for some speculation. ITT watchers see everything from creeping disaster to a gradual decen-

tralization of the company. If there is an end to the rolling
growth and profits of the Geneen era, major economies will
be necessary. The staff system will still be there, and the
controls that it implies — but as the astute ITT observers
know, the staffs exist primarily to reinforce what Geneen
feels he wants to do. There have been very few times, in
anyone's memory, when a staff recommendation has been
made which opposed a Geneen policy. Such a system may
be obsolete or redundant in a post-Geneen administration.
ITT operations people bide their time, feeling that the
company will decentralize eventually and the priority
position now occupied by the staff will shift to the line.
When the pendulum swings, the line managers say, it will
swing all the way. And they have been knitting a lot of
staff names in their scarves while waiting patiently to hear
the guillotine fall.

At the Last Erection

WE STOOD on the icy, frozen New York street corner and bought hotdogs from a pushcart vendor. Deighan splashed mustard, relish, ketchup, and onion liberally all over his.

"These were better when I was growing up," he said. "This corner has gone downhill. The peddler used to put out a good product."

"Tastes pretty good to me," I said.

"They make a bundle on these. Really clean up, don't you?" Deighan said to the Puerto Rican operating the push cart. The brown man chuckled and shook his head.

"The profit margin on these things is about five hundred percent. But still they're the best goddam hotdogs in the world."

We picked up a company fleet car and drove across the city and through the Holland Tunnel to New Jersey.

"Nutley is the home base for the Defense Space Group," Deighan said. "The Cable Division has leased some space in their buildings. Cheap. They just canned a bunch of top brass and we'll reside in all their grand trappings."

Off the turnpike we drove through a squalid section of Nutley to a golf course overbuilt with office buildings and box-like manufacturing plants. The main section clustered around the periphery of an imposing clubhouse compound of brick and gabled houses, tennis courts, and an Olympic-sized swimming pool.

"Used to be one of the best golf courses in these parts," Deighan said. "Probably will make the greatest housing development in Jersey when ITT decides to pull out."

We parked in front of the main administration building. To the right of the building was a ten-story steel tower with what appeared to be an observation bubble, glass-enclosed, at the top.

"One of our previous chiefs thought this place should look like a college. He built the tower and put in the fish pond, but the old bastard died before he could do very much more about the architecture of the rest of the place. The tower is referred to as his last erection."

"What does it do?"

"Who knows? Nothing functional. There are some meeting rooms in the bulge on top. I guess you can sit up there and look down at the world and feel superior. The view is great — all the way from the New York slums to the polluted New Jersey rivers on a clear day. Quite an experience."

We registered with the security guard in the lobby.

"I've got to make my peace with Valente's axe man," Deighan said. "Do you want to come along, or would you rather be spared watching me grovel?"

"Let's go." I said. "Never miss an opportunity ω witness a humiliation."

"This son-of-a-bitch Banino has been around the company for about twenty-five years. For my money he's made every mistake in the book. So the fact that he's still here tells you something. The guy is absolutely ruthless. Never tangle with him, on any basis."

"Quite a recommendation," I said.

"Right. Particularly when you consider that we are both Fordham graduates," Deighan said.

Banino's office was hung with two impressive French impressionist paintings. His bullet-shaped head was bald, and his face looked as though it had been scarred in the ring. His most pleasant expression seemed to be a grimace. I admired the paintings.

"Are they originals?"

"Bet your ass they are. Sent over from New York years ago when Geneen first came aboard," he cackled. "Wanted to impress us, I guess. I think the rest of them were shipped back, but I hung on to these. I think they're restful."

The socializing over, we got down to business.

"Now, what the hell do you guys want? Let's get to it," he said.

Deighan outlined the navy contract meetings we had just attended in Washington and the construction schedule for the San Diego plant.

"We're in trouble," he said. "Our program is dragging — we're about three months behind Geneen's time table and a year behind the navy's CAESAR program requirements. We're supposed to start plant construction next week, and we can't even get site approval from the North American Staff."

"So, what the hell do you want me to do about it? You

want me to go down to Washington and pound the pavement for you — or go over to Park Avenue and set Geneen
straight?" Banino said.

"I was hoping you'd get your boss the vice president
more involved," Deighan said.

"He's a busy man," Banino said. "We're running a
$400 million sales operation here, and we're doing it with a
bunch of goddam idiots. Who the hell do you suppose helps
us when we get into trouble? I'll tell you who, we help
ourselves. You guys go running around in Washington
with all those lobbyists and what the hell do you get? I'll
tell you what you get — you get sore feet, a red ass, and an
empty pocketbook. We take care of our own battles. Let
those Washington bastards worry about hanging on to
Geneen's insurance business. You guys ought to be able to
shape up your own construction schedules and contract
problems."

We nodded, suitably chastised.

"Today, everything is politics, politics, politics. This
bullshit is beginning to bother me," he said. "I'm getting
too old, I guess. Time for me to pick up my options and go
home. The cycle keeps repeating. The big contract, the big
plant, the big political put-on, the big payoff. I know you
don't believe it, but in the old days we really did push these
things through ourselves. We had some goddam good
marketing people then, and some first-rate contracts guys.
We didn't have to go around paying off everybody in
Washington. We wanted a program, we went after it. We
had technical people who had the drop on the industry in
every critical area. And what have you got now —"

"We've got a directive from Geneen, for one thing," Deighan said. "It's a different company now. Maybe I don't like the way it's run any more than you do, but while I'm taking their bread I've got to swing this way."

Banino's heavy brows dropped, his face seemed to narrow as he reflected.

"O.K. Call Joe and tell him to arrange one of his fishing tours or something for your Washington customers. We'll kick it off that way; at least you'll have some action going. Joe can provide the booze and frolic and will manufacture the goddam fish if he has to. Give me a list of names."

He picked up the phone, dialed, and waited.

"Maurie?" Banino said. "Listen, the Cable Division guys are here, and they have got some kind of a big problem, let me tell you. I want you to listen to me for a minute, and then tell me where we drop this hot potato. O.K.? Well, like I was telling you last week, if we don't get this construction program up off its ass and get that cable factory started —"

He swiveled slowly from side to side in the high-back leather chair as he spoke. Even silhouetted against the French impressionist landscape he looked like an executioner. As Banino became engrossed in filling the group vice president in on our program status, Deighan leaned over and spoke in low tones. "Aren't you impressed at the power of the old school tie? I practically didn't have to mention Geneen's name at all."

Frank's Follies

"ON THE WHOLE, as old W. C. Fields used to say, I'd rather be in Los Angeles," Frank Deighan said. He examined himself in the mirror and adjusted his tie.

"Off to screw around again, eh? Drinking with the wrong people," I said. "Our brave Irish lad walking through a minefield."

"Ah, where is your sense of adventure?" Deighan asked.

"With San Diego promoters I have none," I said. "Nickel and dime politicians, It's a one-sided game. Nothing to con them out of except a little good will and some action. On the other hand these finks are a most willing pipeline back to our mutual bosses in New York. Should your fluid tongue announce where all the bodies are buried our chiefs will know by tomorrow by noon. There is no persuading you to go slow on the gargle and retire early, I suppose?"

"Worry yourself not, I can handle the evening activities. I'm renting my first Cadillac as an ITT vice president, Frank's Fleetwood to Los Angeles." Deighan sprawled in a chair and picked up the *San Diego Union*.

"That son-of-a-bitch Nader," he said. "He's really hot on his trail."

"Whose trail?" I said.

"The trail of Dr. Fu Manchu. Our supreme number one boy, Geneen. He was beating his ass up in Connecticut and now he's doing the same thing in Washington over this Hartford merger. Nader's Raiders, they probably will print bubble gum cards in their honor. The guy gives me a kick. I can't for the life of me figure his angle."

"Maybe he doesn't have one." I said. "Honest Ralph, the consumer's friend."

"Impossible. Everybody is pitching for something. I used to think that he wanted to be president, but he doesn't seem to be working that side of the street anymore. That consumer's follies bit was great, telling the housewife that the baby oil company was screwing her, the ditch diggers that the beer companies were ripping them off. But this campaign against big business, General Motors, ITT, IBM — that crap is a bit sophisticated for a wide vote appeal. The flatfoot potbelly in the street doesn't understand what the hell the whole thing's about, not on the level where the votes really pile up. And his war chest will be pretty small, when and if he is ever nominated."

"There could be one straight guy," I said. "He may not be on an electioneering kick."

"Outside of a monastery, you'll never convince me that where there is smoke there is not motive," Deighan said. "Every politician and businessman and super-patriot and gold-star mother I've ever met has had an angle. So I don't exclude Ralphie Nader or his Raiders. But, anyway, they are really burning Geneen's ass and that's kind of fun to watch. No one has pushed him so hard and so long — and lived to tell the tale."

He looked at his watch. "Well, since I can't talk you into a yearning for the bright lights of the Strip, it's time for me to push along. I'll drive back down Monday. Give me a call at the hotel if anything untoward develops."

"Do me a favor and stop passing yourself off as the mayor of National City."

"Why? I'll bet the Okie plowboy enjoys getting an occasional interesting piece of mail," Deighan said. "Well, my boy, Cadillacs away. Ah, if only the old gang from the candy store could see me now. Brooklyn's loss is L.A.'s gain."

CAESAR

When the command was relayed that Geneen wanted the navy's CAESAR antisubmarine program for ITT, all the senior vice presidents in the chain of command replied, "Yes, sir." And so did the group vice presidents. It was three drops down the organizational chart before a division vice president said, "The bastard is crazy." He was one of the few with any CAESAR program experience in the company.

There was a time when CAESAR was so hushed up that even the program title could not be used except in classified references. Then, slowly, the information leaked out and occasional references appeared in the electronic industry press. Finally in the early seventies it was receiving some attention — a few vague articles were published in the popular press and the military information services wrote CAESAR profiles. Naval Intelligence still clipped and noted for follow-up every mention of the program, no matter how vague or from what source.

CAESAR is a series of acoustic listening stations, positioned atop selected mounds on the ocean floor. The system, scattered around the world, uses the principle of superior propagation of sound in the heavy water density at great ocean depths to listen to ship signals generated thousands of miles away. In effect, the system wires the ocean for sound detection, and functions in much the same manner as the radar detector or radio receiver. The signals are picked up by hydrophones, acoustic listening devices streamed along the bottom of the ocean for hundreds of miles, and connected by underwater cables back to shore data processing stations. Information is dumped into sophisticated computers for analysis and the result is a continuous plot of all surface and subsurface activity in most of the critical shipping areas of the world. Detection depends on acoustic transmission properties: weather, subterranean upheavals, and the like. But, given favorable conditions, the movements of submarines and surface vessels in the areas monitored may be obtained by simply pushing a button at any one of the shore-based intelligence stations. With CAESAR listening there are few secrets left on or under the seas.

The technical miracle involved in CAESAR was developed by the Western Electric Company and the Bell Telephone Laboratories, simply by conducting one of Bell's "What if . . . " experiments and coming up with the equivalent of the transistor. Western Electric made the information available to parent AT&T who offered the technology as an oceanographic program to the navy. Like so many other major breakthroughs it was entrusted initially to a small select program group to develop. The navy program manager and the Western Electric and AT&T personnel assigned to the program stayed on, and on, and on. They jealously guarded the program's technical secrecy, funding, special mission, and of course their own positions.

CAESAR grew and grew. By 1970, when ITT's interest was fully aroused, the government had invested billions in the program, still with very little publicity. Contractors were selected by Western Electric and, by and large, were sole source suppliers, their positions in the program carefully guarded by security classification. Unwanted potential suppliers were excluded since they could not prove a "need to know" and technical specifications to bid were closely-kept secrets.

Such symptoms of covert activity and an unwillingness to share the procurement pie were not so unusual in military program development. What was unusual in the case of CAESAR was the extraordinary success of the program group in holding off the competitors and the curious. Usually by the time the cream has been skimmed from the first two or three systems, the great military contracting fraternity has learned the ins and outs of how to crack a secret program procurement and the military must throw it open to bid, like it or not. But in the case of CAESAR, Western Electric retained the program management and never allowed even a peek at their technology. Captain Joe Kelly, USNR navy program manager, was provided with a shadow cabinet by Western Electric to take care of all his technical and administrative wants, something the navy budget could never have done. As a consequence Kelly managed to retain tight authority for CAESAR, and all important underwater surveillance missions within the navy. The program was a prime example of the maxim that with enough brains, money, and time any mission could be performed by the U.S. military-industrial complex in a superlative manner. CAESAR had had all three since its inception.

ITT first looked at the CAESAR program as a Defense Space Group fancy — a passing interest in moving into the antisubmarine warfare systems business. A second look at the program by division marketeers resulted in abortive attempts at selling some underwater cable. But as rumors reached Geneen that AT&T and Western Electric were facing the unpleasant prospect of a forced withdrawal from their military commitments, CAESAR became an ITT prime target. The prospect of selling into a Western Electric–created vacuum, coupled with the chance to establish ITT in an important military communications role, was heady stuff.

"Maybe. Just maybe, Western Electric and AT and T top brass and the whole Baltimore and New York senior executive crew want to move out of the defense business," Charley Farwell, ITT's Western Electric "retread" observed. "But let me assure you that none of their professionally esteemed, lower echelon executives, and the lads actually running the programs have the same thought in mind. Corporate philosophy is one thing, but finding someone to fill in for the technicians who have been entrenched for years is another. They can make the navy, air force, and whoever, run scared trying to find heel and toe replacements. The joint chiefs of staff will be camping at AT and

T's doorstep telling them they are endangering the good old U.S. of A. if they pull out. Then see how fast 'Ma Bell' drops SAFEGUARD or CAESAR or any of their big military hardware systems."

We sat in the small bar off the main dining room at the Army-Navy Club. Retired officers and gentlemen and their bubbling, bejeweled ladies were enjoying the cocktail hour. The buzz of conversation echoed all the familiar military jargon. The club was a secure oasis in the Washington wasteland: a comfortable, friendly place to hoist a few or a dozen.

"So the AT and T-ITT war goes on," I said, "with this one of the side skirmishes. Geneen sees his chance to barge in on CAESAR and open another front against AT and T."

"The rise of ITT under Geneen has not escaped the good old Bell System's attention," Farwell said. "Whatever military systems with profit potential Western or AT and T are going to dispose of will not be pushed very hard in Geneen's direction. What with a history of biting the hand that feeds him and all that, anything ITT gets will certainly not be a present. Probably not even conveyed by default."

"Knuckle and skull, I suppose."

"Absolutely," Farwell said. "But we'll hear more of that from our old friend Captain Joe Kelly tomorrow morning at our private audience. His briefing sessions are intimate affairs where such gossip is aired. Kelly will demonstrate with magic lantern effect the magnificent job the CAESAR Program Office has done in solving the antisubmarine problems for the last fifteen years. He will also suggest the foresight of the program manager for all that time —"

"Joe Kelly," I said.

"And allude to the only naval officer competent enough to have held such an assignment for his whole career."

"Joe Kelly."

"And cite the team responsible for finding atomic bombs and sunken submarines, and rescuing us all from Cuban crises and nuclear blackmail."

"Joe Kelly's stalwarts," I said.

"Bet your ass. Or at least that's what you're going to hear tomorrow. And there is enough fact sprinkled with fable to make one hell of a story, no matter how little you believe of what you are told."

We cabbed to the navy CAESAR Program Office next morning at first light.

Deported from Washington proper, it was wedged in a corner on the twelfth floor of a newly completed office building in Arlington, Virginia. It was a long, squat structure surrounded by the skeletons of five buildings under construction, all of them looking as though they might last through the summer, but not much longer. We entered the Program Office amid the confusion of a relocation: papers strewn everywhere, file cabinets marked Secret standing in the halls with drawers ajar, inverted tables straddled by chairs partially blocking most of the doorways. We were surprised that the floors were uneven, creating gaps under the file cabinets which caused them to rock gently at a touch. My smattering of architectural engineering caused me a pseudo-professional's concern about the eventual fate of the entire floor.

Kelly's Celtic personality never seemed much changed, but he had grown older and smaller since my last visit. A slight man, gray-haired, balding, with sharp blue eyes and a perpetual half squint, his crooked smile made him look like the Saint Patrick's caricatures on greeting cards. Everyone in the antisubmarine warfare business knew Kelly; he had been a key figure in ocean systems since the Korean "police action." Affectionately called the Watch Charm Rickover, he was famous and infamous for successful and abortive navy end runs around top brass direct to the halls of Congress when his budget authority or franchise was threatened. He made the most of the fact that he was permanently ensconced in Washington while the rest of the officers managing antisubmarine warfare programs were rotated on a two-or-three-year basis. And of course he had the patronage of Western Electric, which was, in the opinion of those close to Kelly, the sine qua non of his tenure and method of operation.

"What you guys need is a ship," Kelly said in his opening remarks. His squeaky voice managed a confidential tone, as he waved his arms at a wall chart dotted with red and blue pins. "We have all these old rust buckets converted from World War II that we're trying to use to lay cable. You know, Charley — you used to be the goddam skipper of the worst."

Farwell beamed and chuckled. I hoped we could avoid an auld lang syne session, merry times at sea and all that. But Kelly pressed on, a man with a mission.

"Well, when we get into the new programs, these cable ships are liable to go under like rusty cans off the fantail. If ITT really wants to get aboard this program, the way to do it is to build a couple of ships. You scratch our back and then we might be able to do business."

Kelly was inserting this commercial in such an obvious fashion, I surmised he was in a budget pinch once again.

"Sort of an ante to get into the game," I said.

"Yeah, that's a good way to put it. You ante ten million bucks to show us your good faith and put some ships in the pot. Probably you'll make a hell of a lot of money doing it," Kelly said.

"Have you given up on building the ships yourself?" Farwell said, warming to the prospect of an ITT-sponsored shipbuilding spree. Farwell had built the AT&T cable ship in Hamburg a few years back and had developed a taste for such diversions.

"Do you know how much it costs to build a ship in the United States?" Kelly asked. His voice went up a few octaves and he slammed his fist on the scarred oak table. "The navy isn't allowed to build ships in Spain or Italy and get them for a third or fourth of the Stateside price. You can, but we can't. Stateside yards are the goddam highest priced, least efficient in the world. Bet your ass the navy would build warships overseas if it could. The shipbuilding industry in this country may just put the navy out of business, once and for all, the way things are going."

"Not soon, I hope," Farwell said. "This consulting is a reasonably good living."

"But a cable ship is an auxiliary ship. The navy can lease them or acquire them secondhand, something we can't do with a destroyer or a frigate," Kelly said.

Certainly there were problems in running a first class navy in an inflationary economy. But Kelly's proposal would never pass muster with an ITT management looking for sure and short term profits. While he ranted on, I memorized the funding charts, stations, and program details which were posted and displayed around the room. There was money from some sources available to buy a lot of hardware.

"I'm not afraid for the surface fleet," Kelly said. "I don't know anyone in the navy who knows what the hell is really going on who's afraid of the Russian surface fleet. It's the goddam submarine force, the new Russian nuclear boats, that have us all shaken up. If someone does drop a bomb and we start World War III in earnest, the goddam surface fleets will be off the map in sixty days. Not only ours — theirs and everyone else's. How in the hell are you going to maneuver a carrier around fifteen or sixteen nuclear-tipped rockets?"

"Look at what a few German submarines did in World War II," Farwell said.

"Or what fewer did in World War I. The history is there. The problem really hasn't changed that much. We're still talking about bulk logistics moving to support armies. That's what the navy game is really all about," Kelly said.

"And still you have money problems," Farwell said.

Kelly was suddenly animated. He waved his arms at the wall charts. "It's the goddam internal politics. No one outside the navy knows anything about antisubmarine warfare. I mean, let's face it, we keep the goddam boats pretty well hidden. But once you get on the inside, you find a constant squabbling among the five or six top program offices with their pet projects. It's murder, there's no general agreement at all. And I'll bet you think that the best approach always wins. Bullshit! I'm fighting with OP 95 every month for the money to install CAESAR sites. I face these guys who want to drop sonobuoys out of supersonic jets or rig a destroyer with a five-mile-long towing device. And those are the more rational approaches."

"But you win," said Farwell.

Kelly relaxed. He smiled to Farwell's praise and drew from a desk drawer a baseball cap, heavily laden with golden embroidery.

"The Japs gave me this the last time I was over there," Kelly said. "We helped them with a few systems. One thing you can say about those little slant-eyed brethren — they really appreciate people who help them out of their problems."

I examined the cap. It was a dollar-fifty blue fleet baseball cap rendered into a work of art by the skill of a gold embroiderer. On the front it was inscribed, "Captain Joe." Running across the peak were five stars spattered in what must have been the insignia of the Japanese Navy's supreme command. If the United States Navy would never make Kelly an admiral, the Japanese would, in their own style.

Farwell tossed it back and "But I still remember Guadalcanal."

Kelly completed the briefing, obviously a well-rehearsed act which he did as a five-finger exercise. We thanked him, swore ourselves to support his efforts, and took our leave.

"I'll have him down on the boat next week," Charley said. "He's a hell of a lot of fun. Just have to be sure he doesn't pass out over the side when he gets a melancholy mood on."

The next week we took our analysis of the briefing back to the North American staff in New York for review. Alerted that Geneen was planning an onslaught, we attracted to our audience the most talented financial, marketing, and operations people. An imposing group, it was obviously the forerunner of a massive ITT effort. The ten or twelve specialists, experts, and staff managers listened respectfully through the presentation, then drew whatever they needed from a general discussion. The questions were probing, but unsophisticated. The staffs knew little about the navy's antisubmarine warfare programs. Farwell's short fuse burned low a couple of times as he was badgered on technical points that would have been obvious to anyone with program orientation. Finally it was over, they thanked us cordially with frozen smiles and left to prepare their inputs for Geneen's eyes only.

"How do you suppose they feel about all this designing a new CAESAR system?" Farwell said.

"Like Rommel when he heard that Hitler's idea of the week was invading Russia," I said. "I get the feeling that the staff people are not eager to do battle with AT and T. But they would approach World War III or the creation of Levittown Number 902 with the same detachment."

"Get me out of here." Farwell surveyed the debris of coffee cups and note papers on the conference room table. "I feel like we have scattered pearls before swine. Are there no limits to what one will do for money?"

"Not in my experience," I said. "But I may have been traveling with the wrong crowd."

Propaganda

EDWARD J. GERRITY, ITT's senior vice president and director of public relations, was born to the pen. Son of a popular columnist for the *Scranton Times*, Ned Junior attended the University of Scranton and Columbia Graduate School of Journalism, then served the semi-classic apprenticeship as a copy boy to a newspaper man, went into public relations, and finally became the mouthpiece of ITT. Under Geneen, Gerrity was responsible for all corporate relations, advertising, and propaganda. His staff numbered in the hundreds, spread all over the world; his budget was over $100 million. The organization he directed was disciplined and carefully selected for their contacts, communications capabilities, and absolute loyalty to the Geneen philosophy of doing business.

Ned Gerrity played a larger, smoother version of Pat O'Brien's Knute Rockne day in and day out — fight talks, jargon and all. "My boys always know the play. You can't expect anything from people if they don't know what play's been called," for example, was his favorite line.

He could be a professional pitchman, clown, or political enforcer, at Geneen's whim. No matter whom they worked for nominally, all the people with lobbying assignments in Washington and the public relations and advertising fraternity anywhere in ITT knew that they really worked for Ned Gerrity. Directly or by circuitous route they made sure that Gerrity was informed of anything that had to do with ITT's image or influence. He was always consulted personally for advice in major intrigues and congressional manipulations.

At ITT functions he seemed to be host or near-host of the affair. This "good Joe" show he worked at seriously as a model for his charges, the prototype public relations man always way out there on a smile and a shoe shine. Gerrity was, of course, Geneen's confidant in all matters related to politics, propaganda, and information. Within the company, one soon learned that to have a pipeline to Gerrity was to have a pipeline to Geneen, with perhaps a slight filter. As a consequence, Gerrity was one of the most feared and respected men in ITT, as propaganda chiefs in totalitarian organizations usually are.

Gerrity was personally selected by Geneen to spearhead an effort to make the company a household word and establish its identity. Geneen contended that if you stopped fifteen people in the street fourteen people would not know what ITT was and the other would confuse it with the "phone company," AT&T. In Gerrity he found a man with a journalist's feel of what made good press and an ambition to be much more than the corporate glad-hander.

Like the senior executives who hoped to stay close to Geneen, Gerrity learned to be rough and ruthless — but, as public relations head, he kept his velvet glove firmly in place over the mail fist. A study of Gerrity's methods and techniques is a primer on the propaganda arts. During the past few years, Gerrity has

. . . openly and secretly threatened a *New York Times* reporter for her handling of the proposed ABC-ITT merger, even to the point of having her private life investigated to see if any sex kinks could be uncovered.

. . . made it a practice to create supposedly nonpartisan experts in a number of fields who would testify in behalf of ITT's quality or service — or defend the company's products.

. . . personally directed the anti-antitrust activities in Washington and elsewhere.

. . . helped plot a Chilean intervention.

. . . masterminded the series of congressional liaisons as background for the Justice Department settlements of the Hartford Insurance Company antitrust suit.

Certainly he is a triple threat as ITT managers go. To a degree extraordinary even in a highly centralized company, all public releases from ITT were approved by one of Gerrity's managers. The PR philosophy was simple: total control over external communications and the polarization of all mediums to Geneen's philosophy. Far more than other corporate public relations or advertising directors Gerrity carried the mantle of a propaganda minister of the old school. He maintained a part-time spy, "button man," or contact in all important organizations within the company.

It was through Gerrity's contacts, primarily, that Geneen

saw the world outside the company. Even in the wildest tales of Madison Avenue no one has claimed a ministry of information on the proportions that Gerrity managed to build at ITT. But unfortunately, although his intelligence network was worldwide and all-seeing, the visions passed along to Geneen were frequently myopic and distorted.

As politicians and senior ITT managers found out, sooner or later, the closer one got to Geneen, the more one went through the process of Gerrity's investigation. And if their bond with Geneen became strong enough, they earned Gerrity's continued suspicion and dislike. In certain ways no one but the Propaganda Chief was supposed to approach the Leader, and those that did often fell victims to the public relations secret society without knowing what had happened to them.

Naturally, there were many people who feared Gerrity and would have happily contributed to his demise. And he was well known and roundly disliked by members of the working press, notwithstanding his generosity and lush entertainments on their behalf. Washington legislators knew him as a pushy, overly aggressive huckster who reflected in amplification the slightest disturbance of the Geneen personality. And within the company were those who had been singed or double-crossed by Gerrity, constituting his most dangerous cache of enemies.

"That son-of-a-bitch is two-faced," Dita Beard said over Bloody Marys at the Madison Bar. "There will be a day when he gets his, and I only hope I'm still around to see it. I'd dance the Charleston on that bastard's grave."

Travels with Dita

We inherited Dita Beard with the territory. The San Diego submarine cable project was involved in the location analysis phase of the planning cycle. Early in June 1970, the Cable Division's business planners were called to New York for a conference with ITT North America staff representatives. In a casual, folksy way these experts delivered a summary of the staff's evaluation of the division's progress. Objectives, strategies, personnel, recruitment, "red flag" situations.

"Passing to the political scene," the senior staff representative said, "here are background cards on some of the San Diego personalities you will be dealing with. Frank Curran, the mayor . . ."

There was Curran: picture, personality profile, and pedigree.

"C. Arnholdt Smith, industrialist and a close friend of President Nixon's . . ."

"The brothers Alisio, among the leading Democrats, currently in some tax difficulties. They supported Nixon in 1968 . . ."

"Congressman Bob Wilson, Mr. Republican in San Diego and a personal friend of Mr. Geneen's . . ."

He identified, classified, and gave us a brief homily on a dozen San Diego personalities.

"You will be dealing with the Port Authority, Chamber of Commerce, City Government . . ."

Organizational slides kaleidoscoped on the screen . . .

"The people are largely pro-ITT, you should have no trouble influencing them to our policies . . ."

He moved to a regional analysis: economic trends, port traffic, air and freight terminals . . .

One of the personnel cards fascinated me.

"Before you get to the financial projections, talk about Dita Beard. Where does she fit in?"

He paused and looked at us over his glasses. "If you operate in San Diego you get Dita Beard as your ITT Washington contact. No request needed. She goes with your territory."

Stapled to Dita's card was a full-faced photo of a dowdy, oad eyed, middle-aged lady. The coded information described her: age, fifty; no college degree; first employed as a secretary in the Washington office, 1961; previous employer the National Association of Broadcasters; wartime service in the Red Cross; twice divorced; five children; and more.

"You can't squeeze Dita down to personnel record size and have her come across very well," the staff man said. "She will be a big plus for your program. She swings her own way with excellent connections and very unique approaches to solving ITT problems. Dita is our only registered lobbyist. With her approach she is too obvious not to declare. She is an independent operator with one important thing going for her — she has Geneen's ear and makes the most of that slight advantage, inside and outside the company. She may be working for you, but remember she is Geneen's girl with all the clout that implies."

"Why the San Diego tie-in?" I asked.

"Dita is a self-appointed aide-de-camp to Congressman Bob Wilson. They adopted each other some years ago and she has been our principal Republican liaison since, through Wilson's office. You're locating in San Diego, you belong to Dita, by default."

Wilson was the midwife of the submarine cable project, primarily responsible for locating the ITT manufacturing facilities in San Diego. A reward according to ITT insiders. A sales job, according to the Congressman. The deal was made while Geneen and Wilson were on a fishing trip off Coronado, the location approved while the fish were biting and the cocktail flag flying.

Wilson was a twenty-year Republican Congressman with a conservative constituency that sent him back to Washington every two years without much campaign fuss. His senior position on the House Armed Services Committee gave him a powerful leverage in military appropriations matters, to the benefit of San Diego's cyclical economy. During the city's frequent major and minor recessions, Wilson always managed to pump substantial government funds into the area's military complex, keeping the merchants, banks, and real estate developers solvent. More recently he had expanded his political base and was becoming the Republican party's leading fund raiser. He enjoyed his growing prestige and power as the go-between for the Nixon Administration and its many friends in the business community.

"So Mrs. Beard is on your team," the staff man concluded. "Good luck in working with her. She has a Typhoid Mary simplicity that is deceptive. I recommend you adopt a cover-your-own-ass philosophy. The ITT battlefields are strewn with the bones of her former associates."

We didn't have to wait long to meet the notorious lady. Every two years ITT throws a bash in Washington which brings together ITT executives from all over the country and senior members of Congress and the Administration. This three-day affair includes seminars by day and parties by night. It is always a pleasant spree and a legally acceptable vehicle for getting ITT people together with prominent politicians for a little socializing and a lot of hard politicking. The seminar speakers included Muskie, Goldwater, Agnew, and Bayh, among others. All creeds and persuasions were represented.

The highlight of the affair was a cocktail party hosted by Harold Sydney Geneen himself. As ITT president, chief executive officer, and chairman of the board he gave the affair a sort of regal splendor. The main ballroom of the Sonesta Hotel looked like the banquet scene from *The Last Days of Pompeii*. The room was purple-draped and decked out in Roman forum decor. Well-stocked bars were busy in the corners and a fifty-foot hors d'oeuvres table commanded the center stage, with every delicacy the most exacting gourmet could wish. The centerpiece, a six-foot "ITT" in cut ice, reminded us all that Big Brother was watching. The party was as expensive, posh, and tasteless as most Washington affairs, but provided a great atmosphere for guzzling booze and talking shop.

We waited in the queue to shake hands with Geneen and pass through the receiving line of senior vice presidents. The great man never seemed to change. Short, round-shouldered, balding, jowled — he squinted through rimless glasses and shook hands in a perfunctory way. A half smile frozen on his face, he nodded and looked bored.

An ITT Defense Space Group general manager standing next to me pointed to the only woman in the receiving line.

"That's Dita Beard, queen of our Washington office. She and Geneen make a handsome couple, don't they? They look like Bunt and Blofeld out of a James Bond movie."

Dita wore a cocktail dress, dark, with frills and low cut. The style was an unfortunate choice, since it exposed a square yard of her aging, powdered bosom. She was tall, angular, and at this hour listing slightly to port. The introductions seemed to be bothering her; she looked perplexed, as though having trouble with names.

As we moved closer she was relieved from her station and weaved in our direction.

"Here she comes," the general manager said. "Apparently our faces don't fit. Stand by, you're about to be qualified . . ."

We introduced ourselves. Dita shook hands with a man's firm grip and gave us a long, wide-eyed stare of assessment. Finally she smiled in a crooked way and relaxed.

"Are you a lawyer?" she asked. She spoke in a low, musical growl.

"No, I'm one of the Cable Division people. We're changing Wilson's waterfront skyline in San Diego."

She nodded, apparently delighted to meet a San Diego buddy.

"You've got to brief Wilson on the progress of that program — he's all over my ass for reports. What the hell can I tell him, he's heard you guys spout employment figures from 400 to 4000. Anyway, come on over and say hello to Hal. He's interested in this cable deal . . ."

We met Dita again much later in the evening but the sun was well over her yardarm and the conversation was carried on in a heavy haze of consumed Scotch.

"San Diego's a goddam political minefield. Be careful. I've been trying to get Geneen to finish that Sheraton Hotel on Harbor Island for the past year. What the hell he's holding out for, I don't know. But Wilson did talk him into approving the construction of the cable factory, which is a start. Someday the whole ITT corporate office will haul ass from New York City to San Diego, and when they do, I'll be with them."

So began our two-year tramp with Dita through the halls of Congress. Accosting Federal agencies and plotting in Washington bistros. Flying "red eye" junkets from San Diego to Washington every two weeks for war councils and campaigns. Swapping strategies by long distance phone in between times.

Dita was kind enough to keep us continually informed concerning key Washington and San Diego personalities, most of whom she had little use for and a lot on.

"You don't have to find out who the good guys and the bad guys are. I'll tell you who they are. Just play it close to the chest in San Diego and we'll take care of getting some business out of Washington. With Geneen's interest in this project it can't miss."

Watching Dita operate in those days was an insight into the drama of bruising power politics that was being played on the Washington stage. The moves by ITT, Congress, and the Administration were political and industrial diplomacy of the highest order: the company, determined and desperate, seeking to avoid the loss of the Hartford Insurance Company at all costs; the Justice Department, its crusade against ITT cooling, attempting to retain a trustbusting image while backing down by degrees; the Administration trying to maintain an air of neutrality while rooting for ITT and pep-talking Geneen.

The battle lines were drawn with important members of Congress on both sides. As the dog days of a Washington summer approached it looked as though the fighting would be bitter and the decision left eventually to the Supreme Court.

There were ITT people working both sides of the political street during this period. Strong support was being mustered from Southern Democrats, Conservatives, most Republicans, and even among Kennedy and Johnson holdovers where the company held big accounts. Bill Merriam, as the ITT Washington Office chief, was in charge of a sophisticated propaganda campaign among the capital socialites; his deputy John Ryan and the public relations corps from New York played stealthy political games in the congressional cloakrooms, and Dita Beard and her skirmishers kept up a steady barrage on all fronts.

As the drama continued it became obvious to the more astute ITT players that the most effective potential mediator was Dita's patron, Congressman Bob Wilson. When Wilson's influence was acknowledged by Geneen, he became one of the most important pieces on the antitrust chessboard, and Dita's prestige increased in direct proportion.

Dita was certainly smarter than she acted and shrewder than she let on. But she was no intellectual powerhouse; her personal chemistry and relentless drive accounted for her effectiveness. She coveted the role of Geneen's emissary and would go to any lengths to retain her favor at court.

"I've got two things going at any one time. No more. One is Geneen's Complaint, like Portnoy's, only worse. That you know about. We've just got to win this antitrust case and that's it."

"And the other?"

"The other is whatever is hot or I feel is important. With San Diego as your base you rate high with me, and with Bob Wilson. Keep me up to speed and don't screw around and you'll get a lot more of Dita than you deserve."

Dita was often dour, unsmiling, bitchy, and profane. She was at the same time a very funny lady — and not just because she looked like Oliver Hardy, talked like Groucho Marx, and philosophized like Archie Bunker. Her incredible conclusions, drawn from politically warped deductions, were hilarious. Most of Dita's brilliant problem solutions were based on a completely incorrect interpretation of the facts. A near great comic of the neo-prat fall school, Dita unfortunately could seldom appreciate the humorous situations she created.

"I remember a meeting of some Republican strategy group," a senator was reminiscing at the bar of the Capitol Hill Club. "Dita was closeted with a half-drunk, cigar-smoking group of ten or twelve guys. Things got heated and one of the pols was carried away by some reference to Johnson or the Democrats. He started to spout a string of four-letter words. The chairman stopped and reminded him that there were ladies present. Old Dita stood up, looked around and said she didn't see any ladies and suggested we let him get it off his chest."

A California congressman complained, "I'm not shocked at these gals using four-letter words in Washington these days. But when Dita slaps me on the back and calls me some twelve-letter name it shakes me up. She doesn't know how her damn voice carries."

People who would normally have been rankled by man talk from a woman didn't seem to mind it from Dita because it sounded natural. When Dita used her alliterative obscenities to describe people it fell hard on some ears, but it was always imaginative. Dita's success lay in her ability to play politics with men with no quarter asked or given. She swore like a man, drank like a man, and dealt like a man. Otherwise she could never have played Geneen's congressional court jester and private emissary; it simply wasn't a lady's role.

Once the juice was up and she was committed, Dita behaved like a vigilante. Nothing could keep her out of action. A quixotic nature caused her to conjure up dragons if they were not otherwise immediately available. She had little sympathy with the characteristic reserve of the Washington lobbyist. Dita would attack any position with abandon.

"Screw 'em. They're not so tough. Let's go . . ." These were Dita's rallying cries. In an age of specialists she refused to be pigeonholed. She would lobby, sell, or play a liaison bit — and all on the same day, if need be.

But while her battles and vendettas against the enemies of ITT weighed light on her mind, she was paranoid with respect to internal ITT politics. She feared and hated the "finks and spies" who were trying to do her in, get her job, embarrass her friends, or neutralize her influence with Geneen.

"These bastards like Casey and Gerrity are Democrats. Did you know that? Did you know that Gerrity's a goddam flaming liberal Democrat? You see what I have to deal with?" To Dita the only good Democrat was a dead Democrat, and you trusted any liberal at your own peril.

Long before the ITT North American staff had decided whether a submarine cable business in the United States would be possible, profitable, or practical for ITT, Chairman Geneen made the decision that there would be a submarine cable division in the United States and that it would be in San Diego. After that the viability of the project was never questioned. Corporate staff groups armed with action assignments from the General Managers' Meetings contacted AT&T and began negotiations for the moribund Western Electric submarine cable plant at Point

Breeze, Maryland. This was the only commercial submarine cable plant in the United States and one of four in the world, most of them losing substantial amounts of money over the years. Predictably, AT&T was eager to sell and, at Geneen's direction, ITT was eager to buy. The deal was quickly consummated and plans were drawn to move the cable manufacturing equipment to San Diego by ship.

From the beginning the program had Dita's support, counsel, and cooperation. Baltimore, after all, was her geographical bailiwick and San Diego was her "lucky city." We should have foreseen that a sea voyage between the two poles of her world would have seemed an incredibly romantic adventure to Dita — and of course an irresistible temptation to play politics.

The lowest bidding marine shipping company won the contract to transport the machinery from Baltimore to San Diego. The ship picked up at auction was too small and the crew inexperienced. The ITT observers assigned to the operation predicted dire consequences.

"The goddam ship will never reach Panama, let alone San Diego," Charley Farwell, now ITT director of marine operations, said emphatically. "I absolve myself of all responsibility. The metacentric height of that rust bucket is probably close to negative now. The only hope of her arrival would be a month of dead calm and a looking-glass ocean between Baltimore and San Diego."

But though our project team protested, the company was under contract and decided to press on; the loading proceeded and we hoped for the best.

The week before the ship was scheduled to depart Baltimore I was on a personnel recruiting trip to Boston. At the

Harvard Club I picked up a telephone message marked "Emergency" from the ITT ship-loading liaison man. I reached him aboard ship and we shouted at each other over the din of loading.

"Do you know anything about a Mrs. Beard reserving all of the staterooms on the ship?" he asked, piqued at being left out.

"What staterooms? That's a cargo ship, isn't it?"

"There are, I'm told, twelve staterooms or accommodations of one type or another on this tub. Mrs. Beard of ITT has reserved them all. She told the contractor that she was paying the bills and he should check with our office for confirmation. What the hell is going on?"

I sent the man back to his duties assured that there were no accommodations available to anyone and that Mrs. Beard was a fantasy.

Tracing Dita's possible route through the Washington pleasure spots during the cocktail hour I finally reached her at the ringside of a popular bistro. Out of the cosy background of tinkling glasses, music, and merriment the "maître d' " produced Dita on a tableside telephone.

"I've been trying to reach you all day," she said, commanding the conversation from the start. "Get your ass down here, we've got a big deal going."

For several minutes we sparred. Finally she admitted the report was true. The ship had been commandeered.

"It's the greatest idea I've ever had," Dita said in her most jovial manner. "I told Wilson some of his goddam staff needed a vacation. The poor bastards have been running their asses off for months. He agreed. We checked it all out with the captain, we can take Wilson's people and two or three more. Pack your bag, sweetie, on a three-week cruise we can all get better acquainted. If it turns into an ass drag, we'll fly home from Panama."

Where to start? It was 8:00 P.M. and Dita was still logical. I opt for reason.

"Dita, with that group you know you've got to lose a drunk or two over the side before the ship reaches Panama. Assuming it does reach Panama; the reports I get are betting against it. Consider the publicity when some bare-assed secretary walks the plank in the moonlight."

"Balls," Dita said. "I've arranged the whole goddam thing and you can't back out now. These are Bob Wilson's people, practically Geneen's nieces and nephews. What kind of a wet blanket are you, you lousy bastard? Stay the hell home yourself but don't screw up the trip for everyone else."

Dita went on obscenely describing the ITT deadbeats she was forced to work with. With no choice, I held my ground; to back down was disaster. Next, threats.

"Dita, you're going to manufacture a headline like, 'Wilson's Staff Screws on ITT Luxury Liner.' You'll win some reporter on the *Washington Post* or *New York Times* a Pulitzer Prize."

The argument got louder, the language was blue, and I wondered at the reaction of Dita's dinner guests. More threats.

"We'll take the staff people off forcibly before the ship leaves port if we have to — and I'm not kidding, Dita," I said. More insults. Accusations. Denials.

Finally there was a long pause during which I listened to a blues piano in the background. Dita broke the silence. If

Wilson's staff didn't go, no one else had better use the staterooms, she growled. Quickly I assured her that there would be no passengers. No other lobbyists, none of their friends, no one. She mumbled an abrupt agreement and hung up.

We had repelled boarders. But there still was a lingering doubt. I was sure the ship's farewell party would leave a drunk or two aboard to be ferried back from the last sea buoy at Baltimore. But at least I had relieved the captain of the responsibility of dealing with Dita as she led the nightly promenade around the main deck. And the cocktail flag would not fly from the yardarm each morning at first light.

Over drinks at Charlie Brown's the next evening I told an operations vice president about the narrow escape. He was a Dita watcher of long standing; the story broke him up.

"You ruined it," he said.

"What the hell would you have done?"

"The story of the year, and you screwed it up! You ruined the movie of the decade!"

"We avoided the fiasco of the century," I said.

"A hundred miles off Hatteras the ship runs on an iceberg." He was a man having a vision. "The goddam thing is nosing down with three million dollars worth of cable equipment bouncing all over the place, bulkheads are ringing. On the main deck there's Dita with the Wilson staff. She is directing a couple of Greek sailors with harmonicas."

"Iceberg, my ass — one good-sized wave and that thing goes down like a rock."

"Stop crowding me," Frank said. He was carried away.

"A single lifeboat gets launched and a couple of sailors make it away. Over the dark waters they hear harmonicas playing 'Nearer My God to Thee.' The ship gives a mighty heave and they hear Dita's voice for the last time. 'Get me off this goddam tub. What the hell am I doing here?' "

As the evening wore on and the bar bill mounted, we worked out a number of nautical plots, all of them ending with Dita's heroic demise.

A champagne breakfast was arranged to welcome the ship when it finally lumbered alongside the National City Marine Terminal dock. Although Dita helped with the political arrangements when she arrived that morning with Senator Murphy's party, she was obviously sulking, and still holding a grudge. A stained blue trench coat and dirty sneakers gave her the appearance of an escapee from a women's penal institution. Apparently she had drunk her breakfast so the edge of her wrath was somewhat blunted.

"You lousy bastard," she said, delivering a friendly kidney punch, "I needed that vacation. I dropped a bundle making it up to Wilson's staff."

My only consolation was that in dropping a bundle I knew Dita had enjoyed herself as much as the recipients and that the consolation party was an ITT-subsidized affair.

One of the penalties in taking Dita into camp was that you accepted her entourage as well. These friends and camp followers produced an amazing number of indolent relatives and unemployed friends. Dita pleaded eloquently for these waifs and basket cases. She produced "brave Hungarian freedom fighters" who turned out to be unemployed

U.S. gypsies. The hippy nieces and nephews of her favorite congressional people were proposed for hire. In desperation, we did accommodate her by hiring a few blue-collar workers who were fairly easy to place. The fifty-year-old brother-in-law of a House Committee chairman was a more difficult matter. His career had been spent as a sometime security guard. At the time we had no plants and, consequently, no need to make them secure. To promote congressional relations we hired the brother-in-law, bought him a badge, and invited him to write a security program to cover the first five years of the Division's operations. He got the point and we saw very little of him in the following months.

Dita's office handled a heavy traffic in political barter. She held the ITT grab bag in which there were many prizes for friends of the company. Trips to anywhere on one of the ITT private jets, fishing junkets in the Bahamas, golf weekends at ITT private courses, vacations at ITT hunting preserves, and a host of other goodies, all available through Dita for cooperative people.

Dita was required to coordinate these giveaways with other ITT Washington lobbyists who had important clients to please. But Dita's people seemed to make out best. Not only did she offer them a high priority on what was available from the corporate kitty, she was resourceful enough to call on individual ITT companies when the corporate schedule was heavily booked. It was a rare division president who refused an invitation to pick up a weekend golf check for the privilege of playing with a United States senator, or even a humble congressman, for that matter.

Dita's friends made all the big scenes. They had the best seats at the Kentucky Derby, the Indianapolis 500, the Army-Navy Game, the Super Bowl. The job of keeping up with all of the deals and appointments was a major logistics operation which Dita supervised with surprising efficiency. Occasionally a clerical foul-up would place a senior ITT vice president and a lowly marketing manager in the same Burning Tree foursome, but such gaffes were rare. Dita operated the political dole with imagination and dispatch.

Most lobbyists were happy to keep Congress in a pro-business mood. Dita insisted that Congress, to a man, be pro-ITT. To this end she was willing to wheel, deal, and negotiate. She simply considered it the American way.

Executives' offices are supposed to be a reflection of their personalities. Dita's was located in a far corner of the Washington ITT Building, comfortable and removed from the general hubbub. The decor and trappings were conservative. Citations and plaques covered the walls, together with a collection of photographs of Administration and congressional personalities, past and present. These political graphics seemed an impressive comment on Dita's career. However, on closer inspection one found that the expensively framed credentials proclaimed that Dita was an Honorary Kentucky Colonel, a Turtle, or a Daughter of the Mystic Ladies of the Elephant. The photographs contained flowery phrases and cryptic comments. The wall space of honor was assigned to a famous Republican senator whose silver mane and toothy smile beamed down on Dita. "To Dita Beard," the photogenic legislator had scrawled. "You have a great boss. Sincerely . . ."

The reading material provided for her visitors consisted of a collection of travel guides and atlases. I could never decide whether Dita was planning her escape or thought of her guests as cosmopolites with a taste for foreign travel.

Dita became a minor legend in her own time. At one time or another, I heard from her Washington associates that she had worked as a model, as a Red Cross ambulance driver, as a cowgirl with an eye like Annie Oakley, as Nixon's confidante in his early years, as a foreign correspondent, and in other occupations, all flamboyant. Dita's own versions of her career were always the most lurid and convincing. She spun a yarn like an old sailor. When Dita warmed up after the third round of drinks the truth became much stranger than fiction.

An army brat, the daughter of a colonel, she spent her early years bouncing between the posts of the pre–World War II army circuit. Her decision not to follow in her father's footsteps was a loss to the WAC's: Dita was cast in the same mold as the Russian women soldiers who clobbered the Nazis (as vividly portrayed in old war movies).

She was married twice but neither marriage stuck. Dita was raising the offspring of both, three boys and two girls, in a quiet, pleasant Virginia suburb. Few ITT people saw the family side of Dita, but the kids were bright, good-looking, well-educated, and they obviously adored their mother. Dita took motherhood in stride, as she did her other activities; it was all just part of her Renaissance personality.

Her second office was the Capitol Hill Club, a private Republican watering-hole close to the House and Senate office buildings. The club's membership included all the right Republicans. Here the politicians could unwind, converse, plot, and scheme without fear of too much surveillance from the outside world. Dita was a club habituée, one of the characters in residence who added a measure of earthy humor to the parties and affairs. There was always a Dita story making the rounds at the bar. She knew all the club members and the Republican party chiefs from the hinterland who used the club during visits to Washington.

Dita's special drinking table was at the far end of the cocktail lounge, under the paintings of Dwight and Mamie Eisenhower — near the piano and next to the bar. From this vantage point Dita watched the comings and goings from the dining room, main bar, and conference room. Spotting her prey entering or emerging, Dita would swoop down and arrest him with one of her obscene salutations, pumping his hand in the best ward healer tradition and transacting a little business "on the fly."

"I try not to catch them on the way to the men's room," Dita said; "otherwise they're fair game."

It was amusing to watch her maul and handle the congressional elite. Charley Farwell once accused Dita of goosing a midwestern senator while shaking hands with one of his guests in a remarkable variation of the Irish Switch. She denied it, but may have been too preoccupied to notice.

You could learn a lot from Dita. She had been through Democratic and Republican administrations and had survived and prospered under both. Long ago she had outgrown the duty luncheon and cocktail party routine; she never wasted time at the conferences and meetings where many Washington representatives spin their wheels. Dita knew whom she had to know and, in most cases, she knew them very well, warts and all. As a keen student of the official and unofficial Washington power structure, she anticipated its workings and knew how to manipulate it for the company's benefit.

Dita was candid about her role as a broker. She represented ITT in the process of trading votes, favors, and people. Her job was to head off situations adverse to ITT in Congress and the Administration before they turned into legislation or appointments. The coin of the realm was the tip-off, the payoff, and the introduction. A favor for Dita went into the record books for repayment, on demand, from the bank called ITT.

Dita got her kicks from the character she created: the hard, aggressive lobbyist. She enjoyed violating the social mores of Washington society and scrambling over the ITT pecking order to counsel Geneen. She dealt with the toughest male competition, gave no quarter, and somehow managed to get the job done.

As a Geneen disciple she became involved in the company's antitrust case with a religious fervor. "I've got to protect Geneen from himself," she said. "He talks too much and doesn't know a goddam thing about what goes on down here."

In the early spring of 1971 there were extensive negotiations in progress between the company and the Justice Department lawyers. Dita grew more frustrated and uptight by the day. She cursed the diabolical trustbusters. On the

slightest provocation she would deliver a diatribe, the story
of poor Harold Geneen's persecution by McLaren, the Justice Department's prosecutor, and that "crummy bunch."
As ITT executives in hordes shuttled between New York
and Washington for covert conferences Dita continued to
lose confidence. The government would win in the Supreme Court, she said, the company would be partitioned
and Geneen would go the way of the American Indian at
the hands of an ungrateful government. As a harbinger of
doom Dita was very convincing.

Then as spring turned into summer, things began to
change. The information from Dita's pipeline brightened
her up. The ITT stockholders meeting was scheduled for
San Diego. There was talk of having the Republican National Convention in San Diego at Nixon's request. The
Justice Department's stand was rumored to be "negotiable"
and an air of confidence permeated the ITT Washington
Office.

Except for the comic relief provided by Dita's costume,
a purple jump suit atop open-toed shoes with spike heels,
the conference was a study in unrelieved boredom. We
were in Congressman Wilson's office in the Rayburn Building listening to a briefing on navy contracts. While Farwell
dozed, I examined the collection of GOP memorabilia
which hung all over the office walls and covered the table
tops. There were elephants of every shape and size and
statues and plaques from grateful recipients of Wilson's
favors. The meeting finally wound down, Dita concluding
the question and answer period. We shook hands and began
to leave when Dita motioned Farwell and me back into the
room.

"I want to talk about the convention," Dita said.

Before the meeting we had talked to Wilson about his efforts in San Diego to line up support for the Republican convention. In spite of Geneen's prospective personal pledge of $400,000, Wilson said he was having trouble with the natives. The businessmen were still afraid of rowdy convention politics and concerned about putting a hole in the middle of the lucrative tourist season. But he hinted there was something going on at "higher levels" that might straighten things out.

"The confidence of the Purple Flash here notwithstanding," Wilson said, nodding at Dita, "This convention business is still up in the air."

That was Dita's cue. She reached into her handbag and produced a scratch pad covered with scribbles. With a triumphant smile she handed it to Wilson.

"Now what do you think of your goddam convention?" She beamed at us, winked, and nodded at Wilson, who was reading the paper in a growing state of astonishment.

"Where the hell did you get this information?"

"Surprised?" Dita chortled. "That's the deal. It's from the White House direct. The Justice Department's decision, blessed by one and all."

Wilson shook his head and handed the paper back to Dita who flashed it at us. The names of several ITT companies were listed, dollar figures and notes that meant nothing to me.

"That's it. We get to keep Hartford, get rid of a couple of losers like Avis and Canteen, and agree to some Mickey Mouse about an acquisition policy. But Christ, Geneen would rather have the cash anyway." Dita was in a state of high excitement.

"Who have you told about this?" Wilson asked.

"Nobody, nobody but Geneen — and Gerrity was with him." She was Dita triumphant.

The meeting participants standing at the door were edging back to within earshot. Wilson guided us farther back into the office.

"I'd keep this to myself, Dita," he said; "that's a red hot piece of paper you've got there."

She assured Wilson that Geneen would thank him personally. She left with us, philosophizing that antitrust settlements "sometimes turn out okay when the right people get into the act."

We went our separate ways, promising to meet at the Capitol Hill Club for cocktails.

"Do you think her information is for real?" Farwell asked.

"I don't know, that's the fifth version of the proposed settlement I've heard in the past month," I said. "But Wilson was obviously impressed, so maybe there is something to it."

Neither Farwell nor I felt our fortunes were deeply involved in the settlement of the antitrust case or the location of the GOP convention. We had not been through Dita's two-year total immersion in such problems.

Dita's mood of victory was short-lived. At the appointed hour we met her at the club. She was seated under the Eisenhower painting, sober and upset. She motioned us into chairs and absently ordered a round of Dita specials, double-strength Bloody Marys with "special" ingredients. In deference to her mood, we drank in silence. Finally, she finished her drink, leaned forward, and in a hoarse whisper told us her sad story.

"I lost the goddam scratch pad," she said, "or someone stole it from me, I don't know which. That information is floating around Washington right this minute."

A blockbuster. Hilarious. Farwell and I began to laugh, but Dita's savage glare convinced us to adopt a more concerned attitude.

"I met some of Wilson's buddies and we hopped a few bars. I don't think I opened my bag except to buy drinks. When I looked for it later on, the pad was gone."

The hand of fate. ITT compromised, the Justice Department agreement lying around on the floor of some cocktail lounge, waiting to be picked up and read by anyone.

"With my luck," said Dita, "the goddam pad will be found by Ralph Nader."

After several rounds of drinks Dita was less apprehensive. We convinced her that the notes would be incomprehensible to all but a small group of insiders.

"I couldn't decipher the thing myself," I said. "Unless it turns up at the FBI or CIA, you have nothing to worry about."

We advised her to tell no one about the loss.

Dita's White House information and her call to Geneen without reporting to her Washington boss leaked the next day. The suspect was an ITT representative at Wilson's meeting who overheard enough to piece things together. Bill Merriam called New York and demanded to know from Gerrity why he had been left out. Fireworks followed. When we saw Dita next she had just come from Merriam's office — bloody but unbowed. She had identified the fink who had leaked the information and swore that she would get even with him at all costs. She told us Gerrity had called and threatened to cashier her immediately if there were any more foul-ups.

"Geneen's mad, Gerrity's scared, and Merriam won't listen to me — he's probably sobbing into a goddam handkerchief in his office right now." She looked reflective. "But it could be worse, they don't know about the goddam scratch pad — and that's something."

The information concerning the Justice Department's decision to settle the ITT case spread quickly among the ITT top echelon in New York. Within a week it was cocktail party conversation. The potential impact of the settlement was well enough understood by the ITT executives, several of whom quietly disposed of substantial ITT stockholdings in anticipation of a temporary price dip. When the announcement finally was made the stock lost seven points in two days.

And so we leave Dita at the zenith of her prestige for the moment. The world was a sunny place for ITT in the summer of 1971; Nixon was to have his convention in San Diego and Geneen his favorable antitrust settlement. Congressman Wilson was given full points by both parties as the architect of the agreements. Dita Beard was delighted with her contribution to the great ITT business victory. Later on, of course, some things changed . . .

During her confinement in a Colorado hospital the following year, Dita received a telegram from the Capitol Hill Club. The message was poignant; "Dear Dita: Get your ass back here, there's no one to buy the drinks." Dita is considering having the message engraved on her tombstone. In some ways, that says it all.

Freddy's Flickers

FREDDY WAS a most famous ITT vice president responsible for a swinging electronics galaxy of divisions. "Freddy the Fearless," "Boy Genius," and "Super Guy" were his nicknames in an industry given to disparaging monickers. But now Fred's was a falling star. Recently out of favor with Geneen, he was a man marked for imminent eclipse.

His father was a wealthy clothing manufacturer who never let his son forget that he had done it all on his own. To the old man, all corporate managers were bought-and-paid-for men.

"If you were a man, you would be in business for yourself," he told his son. Now Fred wished he had listened to Papa. Fred, Deighan, and I sat in a quiet Washington bar off L Street, recovering from a long day in the Pentagon trenches. For Frank and me it was the beginning of a procurement campaign, for Freddy the end of a program.

"This fan dance today was a sacrificial rite," Fred said. "There's no sense trying to hide it. My boys have lost the goddam ship fire control program. The big one. And that's going to make my friend Hal Geneen very unhappy."

Deighan nodded. "Remember your philosophical rationale. He who runs today wins tomorrow's proposal. Why keep fighting the thing? Bow out and let RCA have it. Make some points with the navy. That way at least the troubled waters would settle a bit and they will keep you in mind for the next big deal that comes along."

"I can't, you know, I just can't. For the first time since I can remember I don't want to turn tail. I really wanted this one. I thought we should have it. I still do and I'm ready to fight the contract award into the General Accounting Office if I have to. Terrible, eh, when your goddam sense of the political deserts you," Fred said.

"You are too old to begin to get foolish." Deighan clinked the ice around his Scotch. "Stop playing the political game at ITT and you can start interviewing for a job somewhere else. Mail a résumé to RCA, perhaps."

Fred looked reflective. "Maybe I want to be one of the great firings of this company. Go out defending my own noble cause. No excuses. Or maybe the whole thing is getting to me."

"Great," Deighan said. "Just go up to New York, enter the executive suite, walk past the secretary, and shoot Old Hal in the balls. You'd be the goddam hero of this company for a thousand years. Fearless Freddy's Revenge would become a legend, and you the coffee-break David. Celebrated every day by a host of nine-to-five Freddy worshippers."

"Not a bad idea," Fred said, downing his third Manhattan. "But there have been other great boots. Do you remember what Geneen did to Mark DeFerrante a few years back?" He turned to me by way of explanation. "De-Ferrante was a guy GE bounced at the time of the transformer scandal."

"He was my chief when I was a GE indian," I said. "Great guy, I remember him well."

"Maybe you didn't know that Geneen picked him as his head man in Europe. Old Mark — just right for the job. He was as smooth as silk. Just what Genen needed over there to lead his European invasion. Bit of style and the courtly manner."

"So I remember him," I said.

"Geneen came over to pay him a surprise visit in Brussels the same week DeFerrante's family arrived from the States," Fred said. "The DeFerrantes were sitting on top of packing crates when Geneen's messenger found them. The poor bastard was trying to get his family settled. No telephone, no power — you know the bit — we've all been through it. Geneen summoned him and he and DeFerrante went to the mat downtown about what Geneen termed an unauthorized absence. Geneen flew back to New York and DeFerrante had the shortest tenure of any senior manager with the company. On the next New York-to-Brussels flight was the hatchet man. The short happy career of Mark De-Ferrante, who failed to stay in touch."

"And Freddy, unless you get back in the groove pretty quickly you are going to join Mark on the long list of former ITT executives," Deighan said.

"The son-of-a-bitch eats people up," Fred muttered. "Chews 'em up and spits 'em out."

"So recant, go back to New York, make your peace, do penance, wear a sack cloth shirt, and fire your marketing manager," said Deighan. "Save your goddam skin, Fred. In two months you'll be back in the thick of things."

"I may be scared and goddammed confused, but I can't do that any more." Fred said. "I know it must be hard to understand, but I just can't hang this one on my staff."

"Really?" said Deighan. "There is a time where it's not possible to take any more crap, is that what you're telling me? At some point the worm turns."

"You'd think for fifteen years of your life and your career that you could bring yourself to do about anything," Fred said. "Well, let me tell you, the time will come for you, Deighan my friend. There will be a time when you just can't stomach any more of the system."

"For Christ's sake" Deighan said, "I just can't believe it. Seeds of revolution. But here's to you, Fred. I'm still betting you save your ass somehow."

Deighan's Demise

Frank Deighan saw the confrontation with group vice president Maurie Valente as necessary from the time he first became involved with the San Diego Cable Division project. Frank was a five-year veteran of the ITT staff wars and a man whose business career had been spent marking time. He was the perennial "assistant to," always in an advisory capacity. He had served an apprenticeship with two large management consulting firms, which made the transition to the ITT North American staff a matter of doing the same old thing in a different set of office trappings.

Frank had learned how to manipulate power without taking the risks of command: he was an expert in advising the players without ever putting his own chips into the pot. In a sense he was a house man operating on the rake-off. But, at age thirty-six, twelve years along in his professional management career, the itch for line authority became acute. Frank began to chafe at a secondary position. He was tired of the froth at the top of the glass, he wanted to swig the brew. So, it was not surprising that the prospect of Geneen investing over $30 million to put a cable plant in San Diego looked to Frank like one solid gold opportunity to make it into the big time in a single leap. It was the largest installation ITT had planned to build from the ground up in the States. The project would command the personal attention of Geneen and bring assistance from every quarter of the ITT empire. Heady prospects. Frank's classic symptoms of ambitious manager on the make developed into a case of job-hopping fever.

But as with all great opportunities, there were problems — very big ITT political problems and pressures which Deighan recognized would expose him as he had never been before in his career. He would be bloodied before the wolves of his own pack. No longer would he sit safe and warm in a remote staff billet, broadcasting messages of encouragement to the troops in the trenches. He had to do battle. No one would come to tap him for the job of division president; this one he had to go after himself — no holds barred. It was the prize or oblivion, at least in Frank's sanguine evaluation.

The man who stood squarely in the way of his ambitions was Maurie Valente, vice president of the Defense Space Group. The Defense Space Group was where the Cable Division project had come to rest after some palace guard tussling and musical chair elimination. Valente had built a meteoric five-year career at ITT by judiciously avoiding exactly the kind of "all or nothing" challenge that this project represented. Rich Bennett, ITT's number three man, after Tim Dunleavy, had deftly managed Valente's

career through a series of important but short-term assignments, rocketing him to a group vice presidency while still
in his early forties. Bennett tried to avoid the Cable Division project for his protégé, initially assigning it to a remote
part of the ITT hinterland where it could have been dealt
with by people farther removed from the throne. But as it
became Geneen's pet project, visibility grew, and when
Valente was suggested by the Master as program overseer
there could be no show of reluctance. Bennett and Valente
accepted the assignment at a General Management Meeting with smiles and an "eager to get started" attitude; an
hour later Valente was frantically searching ITT personnel
rolls and headhunter scratch sheets for people who might
make the big gamble succeed. His first senior appointment
was from the North American staff: Frank Deighan, a man
reputed to know all about project management and the
numbers manipulations involved, sound as a dollar and
loyal as a Mormon — and above all, a good staff man who
would keep the ship afloat until a captain reported aboard.

In the launching of an ITT major project, the first hurdle
is the Project Authorization Request. This document is the
financial rationale for getting into the business, a report
from the project team to corporate top management on the
how and why of spending the moneys requested. The report
has all of the business planning and market research requirements of an operating business analysis — the big difference, of course, being that it is a paper exercise. Speculation comes easy. There is no harsh history to face up to, no
past failures to refute or explain. The business is established on paper and runs for a five-year period in quarterly

cycles — on paper. All of the operating statements and market analysis which must justify the investment are derived from the outputs of a computer program, biased, naturally, by the data which the document drafters select. In the case of the cable project everyone was well aware of Geneen's determination to have a cable plant, and have it in San Diego. Consequently, the inputs which Deighan marshalled from the ITT staffs and consultants strongly reinforced Geneen's conviction that a cable business located in San Diego was an outstanding opportunity for ITT. Favorable predictions lit the computer boards and ran up the flags and played "Dixie" and "Marching Through Georgia" in the same key. Although staff people winced at having to fabricate and filter their reports, they knew that Deighan and Valente played a tough game. Anyone with a negative attitude, as manifested by unfavorable comments, would pay dearly for not going along.

"Garbage in, garbage out," an operations researcher philosophized later. "Computers never lie, but liars use computers — and all that. Sure there was a heavy bullshit bias. But we like to eat regularly. So 'cable is beautiful' we told Geneen. It was what he wanted to hear anyway."

The cable obsession was a part of Geneen's frustration at being excluded from lucrative market areas of the communications business in the United States. He seemed ready to exploit every opportunity which might eventually allow the outflanking or embarrassment of AT&T and the General Telephone system. His fixation on winning the communications war had cost the company millions of dollars. Project after expensive project would be researched, involving long periods of exhaustive study and liberal consulting assignments. Sometimes a brave venture would be launched, only to thrash around in harsh competitive seas for a year or two and finally sink without a trace. Such a project had just had its demise, an elaborate city-to-city communications system for controlling urban center, railroad, and highway communications. After three years of study and prototype development, the project team simply could not justify a financial break-even for the scheme on a twenty-year basis, or ever. The project was reluctantly abandoned, making way for the next big idea which would allow the communications war to continue.

When I was first assigned to the cable project I holed up for three weeks in a plush ITT executive office, took no phone calls, and barricaded the door with an Amazon secretary. I read the detailed program planning background on which the preliminary Business Plan and the Project Authorization Request had been based. I read, checked, read, researched, and reread. Ten years of operating experience in the industry helped me through the maze of data and assumptions assembled by the planners of four ITT staffs. At the end of my confinement I called Frank Deighan to a business parley in Manhattan. Over a good Sun Luck dish of sweet and sour ribs we reviewed the bidding.

"Well, what do you think?" Deighan asked, chopsticks poised.

"Formidable stuff, calculated to astonish and impress any layman. But not a work of nonfiction, by any means."

Deighan nodded in agreement.

"As business poetry, great. Fantastic illustrations. These reports would take first prize in a graphics contest. But when you put it all together some things spell nonsense," he said, "too much, too soon. In a final version of this recommendation to Geneen, who is going to sign for all the rosy profit projections?"

"Maurie Valente, our glorious leader," Deighan said, begging the question.

"And who is going to make it all happen?" I asked obligingly.

"Me, Frank Deighan," he said. "I'm not sure that Valente knows it yet, but I'm the guy."

Our luncheon discussion convinced me that the problems of establishing a mammoth cable manufacturing activity eluded Frank. Or he chose to ignore the real time data on the assumption that the team of Geneen and Deighan could move mountains. Having given my counsel I decided to select a good vantage point from which to observe the battle for the throne.

None of the candidates seemed to really care what went with the division president's job, other than a key to Geneen's treasury. Deighan knew that the critics would moan that he was too young and roundly inexperienced in the industry. So Valente would probably not want to accept the risk of tapping a novice for division president. Let Deighan be number two man, Valente's advisors would say; find an old head for number one. But the only job Deighan could hold was president; any functional responsibility would be impossible to master in the short time available. As a management generalist Frank had to push

for the president's slot although Valente might want it
otherwise. It was top spot or nothing. Hobson's choice in
the power derby.

"A lot of guys on top around here got there by moving a
little bit ahead of the crunch," Deighan said. "Just so long
as it doesn't happen on your watch. Even the big disasters
don't count for much after you have moved along. It will
be three years, at least, before anyone knows whether this
cable project is for real or not. By that time we could all be
somewhere else."

Frank was not without ammunition. He was a management politician of the first order. He knew how to manipulate the ITT staffs. He was a Brooklyn boy who understood the big city business community. He had been able to
win the important ones, the major confrontations — to score
when it counted most. Big money and power had been with
him all of his career; they held no awe for him. Whatever
had to be done to take the prize, Deighan felt he was ca-
pable of doing. All he needed was Valente's approval, however grudging — the rest he would take care of by himself.
A rather simple political predicament. A recommendation
from Valente to Bennett to Geneen and Deighan was the
man.

As the Project Authorization Request neared completion
and the documents were being finally drawn for Geneen's
review, it became obvious that elaborate maneuvering for
the division president's job was in progress. ITT top managers and pros with years of operating experience were lin-
ing up their friends. The legal department had a candidate,
as did the controller's group, marketing services, and most

of the functional staffs. Little thought was given to the nature of the project or its eventual outcome. The job opportunity was in the title and the chance to operate under Geneen's wing. Thirty million dollars for plant and equipment, loose purse strings, and freedom to operate were the major attractions. Management pundits felt that with that kind of support any miracle was possible.

"Deighan may be in the catbird seat," a Defense Space Group operations man said, "but he will have to kill someone for that job. There are too many old debts floating around and too much riding on the decision."

"Don't sell Deighan short — he is a tough man to beat," the North American staff man replied. "They still tell the story at Fordham about how he ran his own campaign for class president and clobbered the son of a Cosa Nostra lieutenant. This old Italian bastard cornered Deighan at the next alumni meeting, slapped him on the back, pumped his hand, and said he admired the guy who had just run the dirtiest campaign in the history of the college. 'My kid had advice from some of the best political heads in New York and it was a disgrace to have his ass trounced by a dumb Irishman.' He offered Deighan a job if he ever decided to get into the olive oil business. And if he had, in my book, Frank would probably own Las Vegas now."

"Maurie Valente himself will have to make a recommendation when we submit the Project Authorization Request," Deighan speculated as we rehearsed the presentation of the report. "It has to be somebody — and if it's not me, I quit. The job or I'm out is the message for the ears of our management. I've tried to set up a private meeting with Valente, but I think he wants to stall as long as possible. He doesn't want to offer me the job — too risky, I suppose he thinks. But unless he comes up with another candidate in the next couple of weeks I may be his only choice. And that is the situation I intend to push."

Finally Frank screwed up his courage and delivered the ultimatum — not directly, but via the ITT grapevine, the most effective way to get the word out early enough to give Valente time to prepare for a showdown. Frank planted three or four versions of his position vis-à-vis the president's assignment in different places to create just enough confusion and speculation for the rumor to grow while making the source obscure.

As the day for the confrontation approached, Deighan became sensitive to the nature and direction of the political heat that was being generated. He evaluated the potential of the front running candidates and picked up the latest rumors for careful sifting. Finally the PAR report was complete and ready for submission to Geneen, lacking only the designation of the division president and two vice presidents. Valente had to either delay the report or come up with a slate of candidates.

"The dogs are on my trail," Deighan said one day at lunch. "There may be a hot candidate in the hopper we don't know about. Or they may just be measuring my poise under fire. Screw them, I'll face off with Valente in front of Geneen at the PAR presentation if I have to — he doesn't frighten Frank that much."

Why Valente hesitated in promoting Deighan was a popular speculation for people close to the cable project, and that was a very large ITT group. It included all of the key staff members in New York who had been called upon by Geneen to give aid, comfort, and advice to Valente in his hour of decision — and people from several operating divisions waiting to be tapped for support and counsel, each with a carefully groomed candidate in the on-deck circle.

As rumors began to leak from the secret meetings and cocktail parties, they confirmed that Bennett and Valente were still frantically shopping for a candidate, but Deighan was the front runner, if only by default. George Banino, Valente's first lieutenant of clandestine operations, was using his close ties within ITT and his rather complete file of closets wherein skeletons were kept to gather a Deighan profile. Banino of the bald egg-head and battered face seemed the reincarnation of a medieval executioner, a man who both looked and played the part of enforcer. He was the only adversary Deighan seemed to fear.

"Banino has been nosing around for weeks, I am told," said Deighan. "That means that Valente is trying to put together a case against your correspondent. An old technique. Starts with requests from me for reports, marginal comments, and criticism of minor decisions. The whole thing is harmless in itself, but it builds up a dossier which can be used in some telling ways, believe me. Good or bad, depending . . . I've played this game from both sides."

"Deighan is bucking for the captain's job on the Titanic," the North American staff members concluded, but they supported him for old times' sake, and their support began to force Valente's hand. Meetings between Deighan and Banino became more frequent. The criticism of

Deighan was sharply drawn in staff meetings. While reports of the other managers were accepted with few questions, Deighan's were returned to him citing errors and requesting comments and explanations. Paragraphs were taken out of context and quoted in management letters that reached Geneen. The assistance of technicians and staff members was withheld. His name was omitted from key routing lists. The chill was on.

Deighan knew action was all-important and he was on the move. At a social function he managed to spend precious minutes with influential ITT managers; in company of Geneen he discussed the project at a Washington party and had his picture taken with the great man for publication in the ITT management house organ. He politicked the staffs and entertained the influential lobbyists. Frank used his wide contacts within the consulting fraternity to keep informed concerning the whims and opinion of the ITT top brass. He planted alarms and diversions. His supporters provided grist for the rumor mill and his promoters beat hard on the Deighan drum. Frank was running scared, but he was running hard.

"The wops are still pushing me," Frank said. "Valente has got to make his move soon — and he has to have a good reason for passing me over. I know too much about what is going on to be left back here to criticize. He's either got to keep me in harness and completely involved or he has to kill me off big."

"It's all politics, really, isn't it?" I said. "What should be done, and who should be tapped, doesn't make a hell of a lot of difference."

"Not with so many possibilities and so many candidates," Deighan said. "What is it they say in the army? After colonel, the rest of the promotions are all political? Well, its pretty much the same at ITT. Maybe everywhere."

Frank's strategy was to confront Valente, and offer his resignation or agree to accept the top division job. His reasons would be simply stated in a carefully drafted document which he would deliver to Valente before submitting it officially. In ITT jargon the memorandum would suggest that without his direction the success of the project was questionable and he felt it his duty to so state and step down — and out. Or in. It was a brash stand, but well thought out and painstakingly prepared. It would put him in a position to take full credit for the success of the project if it was a success. Or perhaps allow him to observe safely from the sidelines for awhile if someone else was tapped for the president's job. A Johnny Unitas on the bench watching the Baltimore Colts being badly beaten, as Frank described it. There were advantages and disadvantages in being pushy and making waves, but the "quarterback-or-I-don't-play" situation seemed Deighan's best choice of the available alternatives. He had to make a stand that suited his creed and style.

The summit with Valente took place. I met Deighan the next morning for coffee and Danish. He radiated confidence.

"Well, it's done," he said. "Valente pretended to be surprised but of course he wasn't. He was well prepared with some interesting counters. My little heart was beating pretty fast but I think I kept my cool. And, of course, I resisted all the bait. He got it straight out from me, either division president or back on the North American staff, nothing in the middle. I told him that with a new and strange management team the whole thing could be a disaster of staggering proportions. It would kick around for years like a time bomb but finally go off pretty close to his ass, no matter where he was at that future date."

"And he said?"

"He backed water, hemmed and hawed, and put off the decision. Told me Geneen was busy and he had to wait for a private audience. Bullshit! But what the hell can he change in a couple of weeks? Certainly he isn't trying to persuade his potential replacement to make the decision if he is stepping up himself. He will have to worry about whatever happens to us all; Geneen won't let him off the hook. So, I'm betting he wants to keep this thing on track."

The word of Valente's dilemma was a matter of great interest to the ITT hierarchy. Golden Boy under the gun. Conflicting stories of interviewing candidates for the president's job alternated with rumors that Valente was reluctantly paving the way for Deighan's selection. Senior members of the Cable Division staff were queried in private interviews, Valente asking searching questions about Deighan, the building program, the business projections, and recording their responses in a sinister black notebook. The frenzy of activity and intrigue was a compliment to Deighan's political acumen. I realized that he had been building the situation to this boiling point for several months.

Two weeks passed and Frank seemed close to picking up

all the marbles, against some formidable odds. Then happened an event of Homeric proportion. A catastrophe in the classic sense, defeat snatched from the jaws of victory.

Deighan and I were in Washington to attend an ITT political briefing and socializing bash. The session lasted three days, leaving the participants hung over, burnt out, and badly in need of a good night's sleep. Larry Farrell, our trusty Washington lobbyist and resident Svengali, had an appointment in Orange County and Deighan wanted to look at some of the site preparations in San Diego. They decided to stay over in Washington for further talks with Congressmen Rivers and Wilson and hop a private flight to San Diego as guests of Frank Gard Jameson, president of San Diego–based Teledyne Ryan and a carousing buddy of Farrell's. Jameson was a flamboyant aerospace personality who filled his coast-to-coast junkets with interesting people in a party atmosphere. Farrell intrigued Deighan with the prospect that Congressman Wilson would be aboard and the atmosphere would be conducive to some intimate chatting with Geneen's old buddy. Unfortunately for all, Jameson was not yet wed to Zsa Zsa Gabor.

Late afternoon two days later I waited on the private landing field at the San Diego Teledyne Ryan plant as Jameson's plane taxied to the ramp. I had picked up a chauffeured limousine with the prospect that we would have to drop off some VIP's and had alerted the ITT Half Moon Inn on Shelter Island for dinner reservations. A security guard escorted me to Jameson's office.

"Tom, you old son-of-a-bitch, how are you?" Deighan said. He looked dazed, disheveled, and very much in a

party mood. The strong used-alcohol scent of the long
plane trip hung over the room. Everyone was apparently
under the influence of the partying at upper altitudes.
There were several stages of merriment, from aged matrons
who seemed to be giggling uncontrollably to elder states-
men hicupping from collapsed positions on the leather
couch. The party was perpetuating itself in the office with
Jameson acting as barkeep.

Farrell motioned me to a corner. "We have to get Deighan
out of here as soon as possible." Larry was completely in
control. A professional drinker and marathon socializer, he
hadn't let the flight touch him.

"Why? He doesn't look any worse than the rest of them,"
I said.

"I don't think the bastard had ever been drinking on a
semi-pressurized plane before," Farrell said. "He was in
bad shape after the second round. In sequence, he managed
to insult Jameson, pat each and every aged lady on the ass,
and spill every second drink."

"You mean happy-go-lucky Frank, the life of the party?
Who could get bent out of shape over something like that,
with all these characters drinking it up?"

"No, this caper was not nice. I think Deighan has been
under too much of a strain for too long. He really gave it
to Jameson, both barrels. Some bad stuff. Then having
polished off our host he proceeded to play the complete
clown. Like spilling a drink on Mrs. Wilson's lap, lifting
the dear lady's skirt, and mopping it off her panties. This
could turn into another bad scene. We've got to get him
out of it."

We managed, with some difficulty, to leave with Deighan

in tow. He was still in a fun-and-games mood, not ready to quit what looked like an orgy in the making. After hopping a few bars we deposited him in the safe haven of the Half Moon cocktail lounge with instructions for the bartender to have him removed to his lodging when he finally registered tilt.

Farrell closeted himself in a phone booth for fifteen minutes. "I sent all the ladies some expensive flowers in Deighan's name," he said. "But that won't get him off the hook with Jameson. He'll probably place his bitch with Geneen directly. I'll have all I can do to keep my credit intact."

We speculated what effect the incident would have on Deighan's campaign. As one of Deighan's political allies, Farrell was concerned. "It depends on who hears about it," Farrell said. "These things can be blown way out of proportion, depending on who tells the story. There is only one witness for the defense, and I don't rate with Frank Gard Jameson for clout."

An expanded, ribald account of the wild plane ride was making the rounds in the ITT New York salons when I arrived back from Los Angeles the following week. Whether Jameson called Geneen, or Valente, or both was not known. However, someone had certainly told the story of Deighan massaging Mrs. Wilson with a wet napkin very well. It had to be an eyewitness account, so graphic were the details.

Although Deighan excused the incident as simply a drink too many while aloft, he knew it was bad for his presidential prospects.

"When Banino flashes me that crooked grin and asks me

if I have been to any good parties lately, I begin to feel a chilly wind," Deighan said, as we ate a grim noon meal at the ITT Nutley dining hall. He was morose, a shrewd man viewing a stupid faux pas in retrospect. Regret mixed with recrimination, making for the worst kind of light luncheon conversation.

"Not the move of a politician on the campaign trail," I said. "Ordinarily one Irishman in his cups makes very little difference, but the timing was very bad to insult Jameson."

"Something like 'You don't slow down in front of the finish line,' " Deighan said.

"Brilliant," I said. The gloom was so heavy I grabbed the check and left.

In Los Angeles a week later I received a call from the Defense Space Group offices in New York. "Urgent," the secretary said. "Mr. Deighan calling."

"*Arrivederci*. Make your own plans. I'm out," Deighan said.

"Officially?" I asked.

"Unofficially, but it's straight. One of my spies saw a copy of a summary report Valente made to Geneen, including his recommendations for the division management team. It seems, regrettably, I'm not mature enough for the job. A suggestion that maybe I lack sound discipline. You know what that implies. Also, the old refrains about some doubt as to whether a staff will work well with me, whether my experience in manufacturing qualifies me. And, of course, some faint praise crap, like I don't screw movie stars anymore. It's the kiss of death. Since I will never see the report there is no rebuttal."

And it came to pass that the executive appointments for the Cable Division were made the next week, as Deighan foretold. Valente assumed the presidency temporarily, "until a suitable candidate could be identified and selected." Deighan left the project to take a business planning position on the North American staff. The Continental Baking Division of ITT was his assigned beat and Frank settled back unhappily into the oblivion of product line management.

Months later I met Frank over drinks at Danny Boy's in Manhattan after our Business Plan Review. He was philosophical about his demise, unhappy in his job, and pessimistic about the future of the division. All of which figured — sour grapes mixed with a bit of bile and a measure of insight.

"I played to win and I lost," he said. "Funny, though — I didn't learn a goddam thing from the whole episode. To simply screw up so badly at the last minute after campaigning like a bastard for the job. I don't even know who finked. Jameson, Wilson — maybe Farrell." Deighan shook his head ruefully. "The story about Wilson's wife and me playing bartender up her skirt was just too good to let drop. It is still making the rounds at cocktail parties. Christ, what a way to pack it all in. Hero of a Marx Brothers farce."

The Best-Laid Plans

WITH THE SAME CLARITY as they recall their first sexual experience, most ITT managers remember their maiden voyage to New York for the annual Business Plan Review. Mr. Geneen's "show and tell" parties take place for each and every division and company in the ITT fold, somewhere, sometime, once every year. The Europeans are reviewed in Europe, the North Americans are reviewed in New York, and other reviews are arranged at times and places convenient to Geneen. But everyone goes under the knife.

The ITT planning process, now famous among management consultants and business historians, began as a semiformal set of directives and guidelines accumulated over the years since the Behn era. Geneen took the system and honed it to a fine operating edge. His reverence for facts and figures was very much in evidence. The planning process was a no-nonsense philosophy of numbers. Every division or company president was responsible for preparing such an annual Business Plan — a book-length document of plans, graphs, financial exhibits, and analyses. The format was standardized for all, even to the preprinting of book covers and forms. The plan was conceived, written, and presented by division management—but it was reviewed successively by all levels of management between the division and Geneen before it was presented to him (personally, mind you) for final approval. The work of preparation was exhaustive; the requirements for planning specialists simply to keep the plan current was a financial burden for many of the smaller divisions. Most U.S. companies cannot or do not support such a planning function or take the time to assemble all the detailed information required of the Geneen system. And not surprisingly this is exactly where Geneen sees ITT's competitive advantage. His managers know the down, the play, the score, and even the details of the referee's sex life in that grand game called business. By comparison, competitors seem to be standing in ticket lines or still suiting up while Geneen puts points on the board. Be it direction, fear, intelligence, luck, or diligence — for whatever reasons, the Geneen system works and the Geneen team rolls up the score quarter after quarter.

The performance put on by division management in front of Geneen during their once-a-year confrontation is the most important mark in their overall rating. He sees and hears them, and he knows whether or not they are good disciples of the Word. During the sessions — like a Pentagon briefing, advertising agency presentation, or political rally — the results of past actions and future pro-

jections are heavily colored by the personality and charisma of the actors on stage. So the production must be
carefully planned and staged to achieve the maximum
favorable exposure in the short time the division will have
before the gathered New York staffs, ITT top management,
and Geneen himself. The mighty have risen and fallen by
the flickering lights of the slide projector and the whine of
the microphone.

It was cold in New York in late December when our division's first Business Plan was finally scheduled for review.
We had been twice delayed, confirming our suspicions that
the staffs were saving their best chance at a massive humiliation to the last. There was black slush on the ground,
and the sky was the color of old lead. We huddled in a
mid-Manhattan Hamburger Heaven, catching a quick,
pre-lunch meal which we felt might be our last of the day.
The division was scheduled to be "on" at four in the
afternoon, so what with preparation, waiting in the wings,
the presentation, and an interrogation the day would be
filled, with no time for the niceties of dining. Binks, the
division controller recently elevated from the ranks, was
shaken. "Have you ever done this before?" he asked Hayden Moore, the acting general manager.

"No," Moore said weakly. "Not alone. I've carried papers
to a lot of the sessions . . ."

"So have I," said Binks. "And given testimony and
wrestled graphs and all that stuff. But this is different. Boy,
just the three of us. And this goddam plan — it's full of
holes. Maybe you guys don't know what can happen up
there. I've watched guys get torn to pieces. I've seen

Geneen scream at a general manager until I thought the guy was going to crawl under the table."

"Let's ask for a bye until next year," I said. "Plead nolo. Or why don't you have a seizure? No controller, no numbers . . ."

The cab ride to headquarters had all the hardy camaraderie of a trip to the gallows. With our slides, graphs, and hats in hand we presented ourselves to the security guards on the meeting room floor and were duly identified and badged. We waited what seemed an interminable time in the lounge, then took our seats in the great chamber to watch the plans of other Defense Space Group companies unfold as we waited our turn.

Rumors drifted out from the Business Plan sessions in progress to the lounges and waiting rooms, alternatively encouraging and discouraging.

"Geneen just said operations cash management is the most important consideration this year," a staff man announced. "Hope your operations cash management plan is sound." He nudged our controller with his elbow and cackled. Binks was now blanched and shaking. I began to wonder what we would do if he couldn't see it through. A year of planning only to pass out on the stage before Geneen. A tragic prospect: Binks lying there atop his forms and ledgers.

"No negative thinking. Forget about the goddam recession, that's the word," a friendly department manager said. "Rich Bennett doesn't want any 'can't do' shit. If you're looking for things to get worse, better tone it down."

Ushered successively ever closer to the podium, we

watched the production with a partisan interest and awe. Geneen sat like an oriental potentate, flanked by vice presidents in descending order of importance. The hierarchy was marvelously disciplined, spoke only when called on by Geneen or the interlocutor, Executive Vice President Rich Bennett. Bennett kept the harangue and monotonous division dialogues moving with questions, invitations for staff inquiries, and an occasional attempt at levity. He did achieve a type of graveside humor, forcing laughs in an atmosphere of tension that was heavy-hanging indeed.

Finally, our turn came. As in the Mad Hatter's tea party, we had been moving our seats closer to the speaker's rostrum and now we were there. Moving to stage center, the middle of the table, we faced Geneen across the ten-yard expanse of green carpet. The Caine Mutiny court martial scene with Queeg on the wrong side of the green cloth.

We had been warned that everything would depend on Geneen's reactions. If he began serious questioning the staff would be on us like a pack of hounds. We had tried to second-guess his curiosities — which areas to concentrate on and present with slide and story, where his chief interest might lie between the political and the practical. But it was impossible to cover all the holes and patches in the Cable Division program. If he wanted our hides he had only to delve a little.

Rich Bennett introduced us with a quip about leaving the good golf weather in San Diego to tell them all about our Silver Strand Plot. We were launched. Slowly, deliberately, we presented the plan. Geneen said nothing, nodded on occasion agreeing with some statement. Bennett asked a few questions of the product line managers on the staff responsible for cable and communications areas. They gave quick answers, referring to the piles of papers scattered over the table in front of them. As the last slide passed, our brevet general manager sat down, looking exhausted. His voice had cracked several times in the presentation and the controller's replies to financial questions had been halting. But it was over and we waited for the decision. Thumbs up or down.

Geneen rose and said, "These gentlemen are taking on some big people. This is probably the largest investment we've made in facilities in a long time." He turned to us. "Just get the goddam plant built and start turning out cable." He motioned to the staff. "These people will take care of the rest. Any questions?"

There were no questions.

"Watch those bastards from Western Electric in Washington," Geneen said to me, "and don't even have a cup of coffee with them. Or the other competition. No matter how well you know them. There can't be any smell of collusion. We may have some problems . . ." His voice trailed off. He waddled slowly across the expanse of carpet that separated the tables, followed by a gaggle of corporate vice presidents. He shook hands with the three of us in what we later learned was an unprecedented gesture of support. Soft-spoken and pleasant, he chatted for a few minutes while the assembled gathering sat in silence. He asked me about the markets, the prospects for government business, AT&T plans, and the program schedules.

"Good work," he said. "I'll be out to see that beach front property sometime too." Then he paraded out of the room, receiving nods and smiles as he trouped the line. The meeting was temporarily adjourned. Then tension lifted like a curtain. A few brave souls lit cigarettes on their way to the refreshment tables in the lounges.

"I feel as though I've just had a battlefield decoration pinned on," I said.

The controller looked at his hand. "I've been with this company twenty years, and this is the first time I've ever met the president. And I just shook hands with him."

"Fred will never wash that hand again," a Defense Space Group staff assistant said. "Congratulations. You just had holy water sprinkled over you, and you will shortly be inundated with more cooperation than you can use."

After basking in the reflected glory of Geneen's approval in the lounge, we packed our exhibits and headed back to the Barclay Hotel. In the Gold Room we began a half-hearted victory celebration, but the emotional drain had been too much and the evening went flat after two drinks.

"What won Geneen over, do you suppose?" the general manager asked, now out of shock.

"We showed a lot of confidence. That's important. You can't come on tentative with Geneen. He wants a team that is all for hard charging," Binks said, now high on Scotch and blessed relief.

"I've got to believe the pat on the head was just an extension of the deal he made a long time ago on that fishing trip with Wilson, our good gray congressman. Geneen was prepared to be kindly disposed to anything we presented. Old

Bob made a $30 million deal for his constituents one sunny afternoon off Coronado's sunny shores."

"I wonder what he swapped for it," Binks said.

"I expect eventually we'll find out," Moore said. "But that was then and this is now. What a relief to have the bloody thing over. Here's how."

And he drained the last drink of our one and only victory celebration, ever.

Shrinks

HAROLD GENEEN WAS SHRUNK by psychiatrists early in his career. They managed to return him to the business world minus a few frustrations and with a renewed dedication to the principle that work cures all mental maladjustments. Naturally, it followed that all management candidates were put through a series of psychological tests before joining the company. And ever after, once a year, the manager is returned to the New York nest for a recheck on his mental processes — perhaps more often if his reshrinking is requested prior to promotion, or sometimes just for a probe, by someone higher with a curiosity to satisfy. It didn't take much to set the psychologists in motion.

The division's appointed shrink was a naturally repulsive fellow, obviously impressed with his authority. A Ph.D. doctor who let you know who had the upper hand and was given to bragging that his reports were reviewed by a select group of senior management people, including Geneen. A real winner, the good doctor.

His tests were variations on a standard theme. First came the personality and psychology tests. Ad nauseam, the symbols and disguised meanings, the pretty girls with big bosoms, the horses plowing ass to, and the gray-haired old men bending over young boys.

"Describe what this picture means to you."

"What is the old man doing?"

"What is the girl saying?"

The personality profiles were exercises for the simple-minded. Since guidelines for scoring well in such puerile examinations had long since been determined, the tests could be completed for amusement. Pick out the acceptable profile by checking the appropriate square: you liked your father a little bit better than your mother; you loved them both dearly; you enjoy hunting and fishing; you'd prefer a bad baseball game to a symphony; hard work is fun; winning is important; war is peace; and so on. Nothing unusual or controversial or, in the case of ITT, at variance with the teachings of Chairman Geneen. Once you decided the optimum pattern for your functional specialty, it was even easier to score well. And by doing so you achieved that extra measure of top management confidence, the endorsement of being a "known quantity" and "one of us" and "an ITT type."

So I was back for my annual mental short-arm test. The psychologist's conference room was small and sparsely furnished. But the colors were restful, the furniture comfortable, and the mood thus set was relaxing. I collapsed in a chaise longue while the psychologist sat behind his desk drumming his fingers on my dossier and eyeing me carefully. The opening gambit was always a rouser.

"Well, you certainly have been active over the past few months," he said.

The dossier before him probably contained forty pages of his latest dissertation on sex among the ring-tail baboons but its size made it look as though it were my most complete biography. He wanted me to feel my psyche had been well studied. And in good hands. The game involved the bushy one playing father-confessor and thereby extracting whatever tidbits of information would make his superiors happy. My hangups and management abilities would be probed for a strong plus or minus of course. He would note with precision my every controversial word. And he would offer me some advice of a general nature — a rehash of Napoleon Hill and Dale Carnegie, mostly. But the main thrust of the conversation was usually to shed light on our division business activities in an attempt to pass the word on some area of special interest to his superiors. I never expected much psychological aid and comfort from the company shrinks. The trick was to get the session over as soon as possible.

With a "just between us" tone he went on for an hour with tired questions.

"How do you feel about your job now?"

"Can you really immerse yourself in marketing? I mean, could it be somehow more interesting?"

"Pretty heavy pressure you're operating under. Think you'd like a vacation when the building program is over?"

Once we passed the preliminaries and he was satisfied I was reasonably sane, the questioning shifted to Cable Division business.

"How do you get along with your boss?"

"What do you think of him as a person?"

"What do you think of your associates? Are they competent, really?"

"Why do you think your financial man is having trouble?"

"Who do you feel is over his head in engineering? I mean, it is a new technology and all that . . ."

Anywhere you cared to stop and expand a point he was right with you. But be noncommittal, vague, or unwilling to discuss a subject and he became annoyed and pressed. So at any point worth making in his report I began with a reluctance and ended with a confidence. Things began to get silly when he asked, "What do you think of Mr. Geneen?"

The first hours of these sessions were interesting, if only to second-guess what information the shrink was probing for; but as they droned on in the phony, semi-confidential manner it was a challenge to keep one's cool and smile of detachment. The interview trailed off slowly and finally collapsed. After four hours we fondly clasped hands and agreed to keep in touch. Apparently he did not recognize the wise words of Chairman Geneen he had been fed all afternoon. He was not the gifted reader of minds his billing proclaimed or else the reprocessed dogma sounded pretty good to him.

I had ducked the bullet again; I had resisted all temptation to play tricks with the psychologist's tools or to try to tell it like it was or threaten or confess or recant. For five or six months, until management requested another probe into the dark recesses of my mind, I was an "ITT known quantity."

My returns to Mecca ranged from Hellzapoppin zanies

through frolics like the *Brave New World* episode I had
just been through. But the best of it all at the ITT World
Headquarters was the Lobby Patrol. In the lobby a covey
of beautiful blondes and brunettes stood, dressed in purple
tights and looking like Flash Gordon's girlfriend Dale.
Leotards and boots and capes and gold insignia. The elevator dispatchers, Geneen's Amazons. I always stopped to
chat with the newest Amazon dispatcher on the staff. Marvelous comic book stuff, like a page out of Dick Tracy. But
all of this was real, from the Doc Savage headquarters
building to the Secret Agent XI police force to the Doctor
Doom psychologist's chambers to the purple Amazons'
Lobby Patrol. Today Park Avenue, tomorrow the world!

Doc Wochos

THE DIVISION had just moved into its new San Diego offices and confusion was rampant. Files were missing, secretaries shook their miniskirts around the office in wild confusion, trying to keep the teletype operating and locate a typewriter that worked. The Marketing Department was caught in the act of preparing a technical and cost proposal for a navy program, about midway between the writing and the illustrations. It was no time for levity, but Vaughn Andrews, our operations vice president, was saying silly things to me.

"How would you like the recent president of ITT Cannon as an assistant? Seriously, Valente has relieved Wochos as president of Cannon. He's installed Consigliori Banino in the slot and he's looking for a place to put ol' Doc on ice. He thought you might like some help."

"Don't bother me, Vaughn. We already have an office boy. We've got man's work to do." I dismissed Andrews and went back to the tidy world of navy jargon and militarese formats.

Electronic News, the industry's scandal sheet, had just published a feature story on Cannon, describing the fortunes of the giant ITT electronic connector manufacturer and the rumored search for a new chief executive. From the early fifties when the company had been the bright star in the electronics heavens, through more prosaic times after its acquisition by ITT, Doc Wochos had been the top man — Mr. Cannon himself. As chief engineer, a senior scientist and later as president, he had been the man in the news and Cannon spokesman since Geneen welcomed the company into the ITT fold. Now, apparently, he was heading for the shades. There were rumors and suggestions as to the nature of the impending shakeup from ITT staff itinerants who passed through San Diego. But such witch-hunting, ITT style, was beyond my interest.

I didn't take our operations man seriously, at least not enough to call Valente and squelch the assignment. So, bright and early the next Monday morning, Doc Wochos showed up on my doorstep. He was a tidy little man, about five foot six, with a wrinkled, tanned face, always grinning. Thick gold-rimmed glasses, a shock of thinning, graying hair. Dressed in mod fashion, he looked like a friendly gnome, medium rumpled. Wochos collapsed comfortably in my side leather chair, put his feet up on the desk and, with an engaging smile, said, "Valente sent me. I'm all yours now. Wochos is the name. Where do I start?"

Short of "get lost," what could I say — he was signed on.

What to do with an out-of-work division president might have been a problem, but to Doc's credit he didn't make it one. His stay with us was one of the more memorable chapters in the division's history. Doc's vibes were the only happy ones discernible for much of the division's stay at the Sixth Avenue San Diego headquarters.

By some nebulous turn of political afterthought, Valente had decided that Wochos should be "placed" with our division until things could be "worked out" at Cannon. As usual in the haste of communicating such revelations, directions were so vague that Doc entered our world with no idea of what he was supposed to be doing, and we had few ideas of what to do with Doc. When queried, Banino thought he recalled there was mention of his assisting us in the area of technical proposals. So Doc migrated to Marketing, the area of his least experience.

Assembling a technical proposal for submission to a Pentagon procurement group is something like putting together a book with each chapter written by a different author. Such proposals range from a few pages to several thick volumes, and often include lavish illustrations, multi-page fold-out charts, overlay graphs — and in some cases, a "dog and pony" show script to accompany its presentation. The proposal we had embarked on was of medium complexity, an effort that included a text of two-hundred-odd pages and a few plant layouts and PERT diagrams. We assigned Doc as "coordinator," with a part-time staff made up of cute secretaries and shapely market research girls of varying ages and sizes to keep him occupied. Normally the job would have fallen to a junior marketing specialist, but with Doc available we decided that we would overskill it by orders of magnitude and let him have at it. It was like asking the secretary of defense to drill an infantry squad,

but Doc's real talents couldn't otherwise be employed, it
seemed, and at least the proposal activity would chew up
his surplus of time.

Coordinator Wochos worked like a madman. He was at
the secretaries' sides as they collated, as they punched, and
as they bound each and every section of the proposal. He
proofread every page and all but put a third hand on the
typewriters. Doc helped the action along with a friendly pat
on the butt here and a pinch there — which, after a bit of
getting used to, the sweet younger and older things of the
secretarial staff seemed to appreciate. Watching the performance we were sure that Doc was in the process of col-
lecting himself a harem. He was away from his Los Angeles
abode, after all, living in a fancy San Diego hotel and free
to indulge himself in any direction he chose. To his credit,
except for a lot of patting and pinching and a continual
round of three-cocktail lunches with the delighted secretaries, he deported himself in the great tradition of the
aging, harmless roué. If there were any *affaires de coeur*,
they were Doc's well-kept secret from an office grapevine
highly sensitive to any "fun and games" situation in
progress.

My education into the *haute politique* of ITT really
began with Doc's acquaintance. As Valente's staff was
busily sweeping all manner of things under the rug at
Cannon, Doc watched with detachment. He was philo-
sophic in his acknowledgment of what was happening to
his business and himself.

"It's all catch-up football after a certain point," he said
at lunch at the University Club. "When the family owned

Cannon it was number one in the connector business. Then they sold out to ITT. Hell, it had to be someone; all the conglomerates were knocking on the door. But pretty soon the staff people began crawling all over the place. From a standing start they managed to screw up the company for over a year. Finally we began to put the pieces back together and we made some real money. I mean, we really hit it. Made millions and millions for Geneen. I was the fair-haired boy, with a warm handshake and arm around the shoulder every time we met. But old Hal takes things personally. When we began to fall on hard times last year things got sticky between us. You make money and you are his boy; you lose money, you've screwed him personally. There are no excuses."

Two weeks after Doc reported aboard I was back in New York at a Business Plan Meeting listening to Valente's staff cut Wochos up one side and down the other. Their recommendations included firing his staff and completely restructuring the organization. The reassignment of the Cannon Division to the Defense Space Group under Valente was made and the guillotine lists prepared. A quiet little execution by proxy for Doc Wochos.

The Cannon problems were really nothing new or different: a losing share of the overall market, reduced profits, and an overstocked inventory situation. No one at the meeting bothered to point out that the electronics industry as a whole was in trouble, and the connector business in particular was worst hit of the component manufacturers. In fact, under Wochos, Cannon had been weathering better than most. It was a rule that the immature electronics industry went through such a blood bath every three or four years, either from economic depressions or simply marginal producer shakeouts. In the past, apparently, Doc had been able to ride the crest. Now, for the first time, he had been caught in the trough with all the rest. But once was enough for Geneen.

I never mentioned to Doc that his former protégé, Valente, had treated him in such a shabby fashion. But the Doc's antenna was well tuned; he found out. It must have hurt, but he shrugged it off.

"We ran into a bad inventory situation two years in a row," Doc said. "Not unusual in this business. But we had been able to shield Geneen from such realities for a number of years. The first time he noticed our problem there were three or four North American staff people assigned on site to watch us. We tried to give them a quick education in the business, but they were bent on recommending one of Geneen's massive surgery solutions. What else could they do, their chestnuts were in the fire and they had very little time to come up with a solution."

"And Cannon moves quietly into the Defense Space Group sphere under Valente," I said. "Bullshit, it doesn't compute."

Doc chuckled, "I don't blame Maurie. Not much, anyway. He did what he had to do. There may be no way to play his part except as a hatchet man for Geneen. So, if he is aspiring to the big time, I guess he has to screw a few friends now and then."

"Why don't you talk to Geneen?" I said. "There's always the possibility he doesn't know what is really going on."

Doc shook his head, "Geneen never hires in person or fires in person. Or talks to someone who has been given the old Mafia kiss."

"Maybe it's time for a power play," I said, "or some political skullduggery."

"It's funny, I've spawned more ITT managers who have gone on to big things than anyone in the company. When I think of the education they've received from me and how they've used it to advance politically, I wonder how the hell I managed to goof so badly. Obviously, I'm the most apolitical son-of-a-bitch around, which is why I'm where I am now."

But Doc did cast his bread upon the waters. He contacted many friends in four corners of the company and received information and advice. From the Siberia of the Cable Division Doc was trying to influence his own fate — probably because substantial stock options hung in the balance.

Meanwhile he worked on the navy proposal like a man possessed. He supervised every layout personally, chased down draftsmen, argued with graphic arts people, and in the process developed the secretaries and market research girls into a dedicated team. Normally a proposal of the type they were assembling would have taken three weeks to write, wrap up, and submit. Doc's proposal team labored for two months, and in the end produced more of an artistic masterpiece than an actionable document. But it was all worthwhile. The effort was a morale boost for Doc, his team, and the division in general. And for me a liberal education in ITT politics, management games, and memento mori.

"Obviously, you're here to take over the division once Geneen decides he's had enough of the Britishers," Doc said. "Unless Geneen is losing his marbles. Classically these European characters stay for a while, then go back home lugging fat bonus checks and describing all their more unfortunate memories of life in the colonies."

Among Doc's graduates from the Cannon school of management was Jacques Bergerac, then rumored to be in line for a group vice presidency in Europe.

"He's a Valente type, or Valente's a Bergerac type, I don't know which. I watched the two of them perform at Business Plan Meetings for years. Bergerac carefully preserves a cracking Parisian accent which delights Geneen. Valente leans on his Italian taste to decorate his slide peep shows in fifteen different colors and puts them on like a three-ring circus. But for all it was obvious that Valente was playing on Geneen's love of theatrics and Bergerac had found a tone that pleased his ear, the flattery worked. On such small bearings does the ITT world turn, with a guy like Geneen on the throne."

As the navy proposal activities wound up, we received vague calls from Valente about Doc's attitude and his activities. There were other inquiries from New York, almost as though the personnel department wanted to be sure that Doc was still in tow and had not escaped. The cryptic phone calls and top executive interest delighted Doc.

"It's interesting, the 'coup de grace' ceremony," he said. "I've watched it happen to any number of seniors at ITT, and my intuition tells me the stage is being set for me right now. I suppose Valente's staff people have already made things look so bad there's no hope of my going back to Cannon. They have to when their own heads are so close to the block. At Cannon they are playing with ten million plus or minus in profit and there's no forgiveness for mistakes. 'Throw out the rascals; bring in new management' is always an acceptable solution."

"So what happens at Cannon?" I asked.

"My middle management people will probably recant and confess that our goals were unrealistic," Doc said. "The situation will appear so badly screwed up that the only rational thing to do will be to reduce all the forecasts. Ergo, all the charts start from a much lower figure. And for the next year they go up, percentage-wise. And Geneen's targets will come close to being met — again percentage-wise. On a reduced scale, of course, not in terms of real dollars or growth."

"Clever," I said. "But isn't that obvious?"

"Yes, but probably necessary in an ass-saving ceremony. Nothing will have changed but things have to appear to improve. So, short of total war or atomic disaster, the guy they pull in to run the division will make his bogey for the next year. By that time Valente will be out from under, the staff will have totally infiltrated the operation, and the pigeon that's been picked as general manager will be on his own." Doc shook his head gravely over his coffee cup, held in both hands. "If they hire a genius or a lucky son-of-a-bitch, he may continue the trend. If he is neither he falls into the familiar ITT three-year cycle, 'cradle to grave for the manager brave.' "

For all Doc's show of sang-froid and humor occasionally

I felt I was talking to an inmate on Death Row. There was something disconcerting about waiting for the axe to fall all the way from Park Avenue. Though Doc obviously knew what he was doing, the cards seemed hopelessly stacked against him. I suggested a resignation and early departure to a new venture might be his best and easiest course.

"Resign! Are you crazy?" Doc said. "In the first place I'm not giving anyone the satisfaction of winning this goddam war of nerves. It would be unprofessional of me to do it. And more to the point, there is a hell of a lot of money at stake in stock options and such that I'd like to tuck away. If they are considering sweating me out, they're crazy. At this point, I'm enjoying the game."

So Doc languished on, but happily. He seemed to be growing younger through the experience. He squired his distaff team to lunch, sported progressively more mod clothes, and was obviously living up his sabbatical to the fullest.

Dressed in bright green and maize golf togs, Doc stumped into my office late one Friday afternoon. He was excited. He struck an attitude with arm on bookcase and announced, "Monday's the day. The super ITT personnel surgeon, Old Frank White, is on his way. He just called me. This is the straight-from-Geneen executioner. A most senior axe man. I've been honored. This son-of-a-bitch looks like Lewis Stone right out of an Andy Hardy movie. Very deceptive and thorough. I've watched him cut guys up into little pieces for years."

"Well, I must say you don't look very disturbed." I

looked for signs of false courage, but Doc was one big smile of anticipation.

"He'll come in on tiptoe, see. We'll have a big lunch and talk about the good old days. He'll give me some choice tidbits of scandal, and we'll be right there on that old buddy-buddy level," Doc chuckled. "Then gradually, the old bastard will move to talk of my career. Things aren't what they used to be, he'll say in a sad voice. Changes are taking place, young guys are coming in. Geneen is getting more and more remote. All that crap — and before I know what's up, we'll be talking about some cutoff date that I should refer to in my resignation. Which, by the way, we will both have come to acknowledge I will be submitting shortly. Out of generosity, Frank will arrange for an executive headhunter to program my re-employment."

"No muss, no fuss, and no more problems with Doc Wochos," I said. "Well, so long Doc, it's been real."

"Not so fast. That's the script; however, old Frank is in for a few surprises. This time the goddam band is gonna play to Doc's tune. I know that none of these guys move on their own. Valente won't have the guts or disposition to fire me outright. Not yet, anyway. Geneen won't fire anyone himself. Who the hell else has the interest or authority? Certainly not these staff personnel milksops. Maybe we'll show them that there's a tussle in the old boy yet. Let's see who has the intestinal fortitude to toss me out the door personally."

Sure enough, the following Monday Frank White arrived with two assistants. They looked like an expensive undertaking team. At Doc's request, I had assigned him an office where he might entertain his "guests." Comfortably settled, they held the first in a series of closed-door sessions. On emerging, finally, Doc was smiling, the others looked dour. Before I could make off, Doc introduced me.

"This is Frank White, an old friend from New York," Doc said, slapping White on his thin shoulder. White shook hands in a perfunctory manner, the calculated single-pump, squeeze grip of a personnel man.

"I've heard a lot about you," he said, nodding gravely. "Delighted to have an opportunity to meet you."

I felt a cold wind; it was like being told by your doctor that you had an interesting ailment.

Doc guided the personnel triumvirate on a tour of the Cable Division construction project at National City. We were all hoping for the best for Doc, but expecting otherwise. Tour over, the meetings resumed and lasted the rest of the day. Seen in brief glimpses Doc seemed more haggard. He had lost his sunny disposition and apparently some of his cool. Finally, it was over. White and staff, still looking grim, said farewell all around and left for the New York jet.

"So much for that," Doc said, obviously relieved. His grin was back. "It got a little bit tiresome towards the end."

"Well, what's the score?" I said.

"By my count, it's Wochos sixty, White zero. After I got a little tired of the formalities I told Frank in a zero bullshit approach that I thought I'd hang around until my stock options were taken care of and I'd collected what was due me."

"He liked that?"

"No. Apparently the message from Geneen was Wochos to the wall — Valente, of course, concurring. But I gave White a message for Geneen, and I assume he's going to deliver it verbatim." Doc was reflective, retracing in his mind a disagreeable experience, probably more cutting than he had anticipated. "It's unfortunate, you can never bring yourself to admit that a company can throw you out on your ass with such abandon. A goddam $6 billion company acting like a juggernaut that's gonna run right over Doc Wochos, crack up his career, and try to ruin his life. And for what? This is the same Doc Wochos that put millions of bucks into their coffers lately and gave them the best goddam connector company in the business. It's foolish, I suppose, to impute anything in the way of human emotions to the guys who run these circuses. But, I don't know, for some stupid goddam reason, I take it all personally. Like they were ungrateful. That's funny, I suppose — expecting gratitude."

"Yes, it is. Not funny, more like sad," I said. "So what happens now?"

"I had prepared a little written scenario for White to take back with him. I told him to give it to Geneen, personally. It goes like this. Wochos could pick up and join a competitor next week. But if he does, every goddam engineering, manufacturing, and marketing program and plan of Cannon's will be public property. And Wochos will devote his declining years to running ITT's ass right into the ground. I calculated a figure for Geneen, since that's what turns him on. The figure is $6 million. A minimum $6 million mistake if he throws Wochos to the wolves now.

If Wochos hangs around, however — picks up his options, has some time to look around, decides on a comfortable place to settle where he won't compete with ITT head-on, then the company is ahead six million bucks and keeps my personal good will."

"Clever bluff, the exhibits and the numbers. Will it work?" I asked.

"It's no bluff," Doc said. "I'm just fortunate enough to be able to make the threat stick; or let's say Geneen can't afford to take the chance. He'll probably kick some asses around out of frustration, and Valente and Bennett will be somewhat embarrassed that I was not a willing candidate for the block. But, when you consider the people I'm dealing with, there are a limited number of ways to protect yourself. Blackmail is one, and in this case, pretty obvious blackmail at that."

It worked. Weeks passed, Doc's bet was never called. He finished his Cable Division assignment and had a rousing send-off when he left San Diego to proceed all the way up the coast to Los Angeles. Doc was made a consultant to the West Coast ITT military divisions, an assignment which involved arriving at his Los Angeles office a few days a week and translating some operations hieroglyphics for the new Cannon general manager, freshly imported from an alien technology. At last report Doc was still giving the translation bit his all and exercising stock options at his leisure. For the period of his consultancy the secretaries at Cannon are sure to be a delighted group, especially if anyone decides to write a technical proposal in the Wochos style.

Congressman Wilson

ALTHOUGH WE COULD VISIT him openly in Washington,
Bob Wilson, our San Diego congressman and benefactor,
preferred neutral ground when at home. One of the acceptable locations for our surreptitious gatherings was a beach
house on the shores of Mission Bay. Quiet, secure from in-
trusion, it was a place where problems looked smaller
against the backdrop of white yachts standing out to sea
and gulls turning slow spirals upward. One Saturday
morning he asked that we meet him at the beach house on
a matter of some urgency. Freely translated this usually
meant he had just received some "suggestions" from
Geneen. We arrived about nine o'clock to find Wilson in a
California blue-slacks-and-sport-shirt combination, comfortably set up in a chaise longue with binoculars trained on
the yacht basin. He motioned us into chairs and we drew
canned Budweiser from a large ice bucket. He finally
caught what he was looking for, made some note on a
scratch pad, and set the navy 7x50 aside.

Wilson was an old-shoe kind of guy, with a quiet, sincere, professional man's appearance that belied the shrewd, hard-eyed politician. Bob had been reared in San Diego when it was a sleepy navy town and had seen the hard old days. He had been a part-time milkman, so-so advertising man, and finally a talented politician without losing his folksy ways or the touch of candor in his style that charmed the press. Of medium height, hair thin, paunchy, with a perpetual sad smile and dark circles under his eyes, he looked like a man schooled in hearing bad news and taking it well. Lately most of the news had been very good indeed for Wilson, but he could cope with that too.

"So what is it you want our appropriations committee to do?" he asked. "Apparently you are having some procurement problems." To the point, as always. Geneen must have told him to "get those clowns in line."

Moore, the acting general manager, fidgeted and looked for me to begin. Andrews, the operations vice president, studied the pattern in the rug. No help there. So I pushed off, trying to second-guess what ground Geneen and Wilson had already been over.

"I don't think we know at this point," I said. "We think that there have been some defective contracts written and passed out for navy submarine cable programs and CAESAR components in particular. The Defense Space Group legal staff is looking into that situation. We are told that Mr. Geneen is interested in pushing the company's entrée into the CAESAR program. Total systems responsibility, if possible. That puts the Cable Division in the van."

"That's a big order, CAESAR," Wilson broke in. "You

know, I am one of the few people in Congress that have
known about CAESAR since the first system was put in the
water. We've hushed it up and funded it as well as any
program I can ever remember."

"Now it may be up for grabs," I said. "We hear AT and T
wants out. But, again, we aren't certain — we may still
have to fight them for the follow-on program. A new technology, perhaps —"

"If we don't get some military cable business soon we
may simply be out of business," Moore said. As division
general manager, temporary status, his chestnuts were
very squarely in the fire. No CAESAR program, no long-
term payoff, no job. "Our New York people should be
worried about getting some navy cable orders. Without
them, this division is dead — now or in a few years, it
doesn't make much difference."

"I thought this had long since been settled," Wilson
said. "Your public relations people made the announcement that three cable plants in National City would be
filled in a year. Three plants, I remember — a thousand
to fifteen hundred jobs. There were feature stories in all
the papers from here to San Francisco. And you did get a
hell of a big tax break from National City. That's something that you're going to have to live with. There are
going to be a lot of questions about preferential treatment
and tax concessions unless a thousand people are making
cable down there in National City next year."

Andrews shook his head and continued his hypnotic fixation with the rug. "There'll never be fifteen hundred people
employed there. Our employment estimates now are about

four hundred, at full capacity. And no one has approved three plants. One plant, four hundred people. Period."

Wilson whistled softly. "Gentlemen, you have a problem. Geneen has talked about some big plans for San Diego and the city fathers are expecting great things from him. And me, I might add."

"To get our manufacturing program off the ground we need a navy contract for CAESAR cable," Moore said. The ITT staff people in New York say they were led down the garden path by the Pentagon. Our Defense Space Group people say the navy gave them all kinds of assurances. If ITT would build a plant and provide a second source for cable the next cable contracts would be split. Now that procurement time rolls around memories seem to be getting short, I must say. The navy lawyers now recall they have contracts outstanding. We need the business now, not two years from now," Moore said.

"I'm one of the best friends the navy has; they'll support me if I have a case," Wilson said defensively. "But you are not picking on the scrubs. CAESAR is *the* antisubmarine warfare program and it has a top priority right now. ITT competing with AT and T and Western Electric Company is fine if you know what you are doing. And I hope you do. In all modesty I tell you that I've done a hell of a lot for Geneen in Congress. But pushing around AT and T, the navy, and Western Electric is a degree of difficulty beyond anything I've ever succeeded at. And if you can't come through on this cable complex building program, with those factories and a couple of thousand jobs, we will have a lot of unhappy people to deal with in San Diego, most of them my friends."

Wilson stood. We were being dismissed. Wilson looked more sad than usual; he obviously was very unhappy with the information we had given him. I could see the perspiration on Moore's brow at the mention of discussions with Geneen. Wilson's report on our effort would not be favorable.

"Is there anything you need from us? I mean, can we fill you in on any more of the details?" Moore said.

Wilson picked up his binoculars and scanned the seascape. "I don't think so. I'll give Dita Beard a call when we get back to Washington and we can arrange to get together." He gave us a wistful smile, shook hands gravely, and tried to be cheerful. "These things are always easier to talk about on the ocean somewhere. Who knows, if the fishing's good, perhaps I can persuade Geneen to buy Western Electric or the navy. Call me next week."

We walked down the pebble driveway to the car. Moore stumbled along in a state of mild shock.

"Moore's scared. Are you?" I asked Andrews.

"Unless Geneen pumps Wilson up to push ahead hard, I'll have the only endless taco plant in the world on my hands," Andrews said, "and no customers for endless tacos, either."

"Oh well, I can always go back and sell cars in London," Moore said, smiling weakly. He was still perspiring profusely. He's not joking, I thought.

"When Geneen gets through with you, they won't let you back into the U.K.," Andrews said. "You'll wind up shining shoes in East Orange, New Jersey. With lots of competition from former cable plant managers."

A Little Action

DITA BEARD had scuttled halfway across L Street against the light when she heard me call. Miraculously pirouetting, she managed to weave her way between cars back to the sidewalk, achieving a Washington traffic miracle.

She was breathing hard. We shook hands and cussed and patted each other.

"On my way out to the Wilson diggings at the Rayburn. Ed Reinecke and his bride are in from your Golden State, convention package in hand, if my information is on target. Get a cab and we'll go and screw around there together," Dita said.

I waved and a cab made a kamikaze turn for the curbing. How often our humble cable program was becoming confused with the ITT global strategy, I thought— today a mulligan stew of Wilson, Reinecke, and antitrust strategy and antisubmarine warfare. Dita pushed me into the rear seat first and slammed the door.

"Nothing like a little action to pick up a girl's spirits," she said. "Next best thing to getting laid is a little political skullduggery."

A Capital Ship

IN SOME WAYS getting word back to Geneen was like writing a letter to Santa Claus. Anything seemed possible if he was agreeable. For example, one day at a casual luncheon in the executive dining room, between the main course and dessert, he bought us the *Neptun*, the largest cable ship in the world. Or at least he ordered it, delivery to follow.

The Cable Division badly wanted a cable layer. We had hung up our stocking for a ship a long time before that luncheon purchase. In memo, letter, and report we had pointed out that the U.S. Underseas Cable Corporation, owner of the super cable ship *Neptun*, was being surreptitiously put on the block by their owners. One of the choice items in their stockpile was the cable ship, of course, but there were others, such as systems equipment and service contracts. The ship was just what we needed for our own cable installation programs, but the equipment would help, too. And the contracts meant cash in our tills, for the first time ever.

But no management buys a cable ship casually, and we

had been through months of haranguing with lawyers, marine architects, accountants, and more lawyers without moving very far off dead center.

"In my book there are two reasons for instant dismissal," our group vice president said. "One is a request to buy a ship. Any ship, anytime."

But even his threats did not dissuade us. We did ask, over and over again, but to no avail.

How Geneen learns things was a well-kept secret. Rumor had it that he read every telegram going and coming from the New York headquarters and all important correspondence. There were also stories of vast espionage organizations and a network of informers, one each to a division. But, whatever his methods, Geneen knows all. And somehow, across a continent and through the management filters, he heard our cries of anguish over the lack of a ship.

Stanley Luke, senior ITT vice president in charge of arranging mergers and buying things, was sitting next to Geneen at the luncheon table on this day when he was asked by Geneen why he hadn't bought that cable ship yet.

"I beg your pardon?" Luke said, now strangling a bit on the green beans.

"The cable ship," Geneen said. "Why haven't you bought the cable ship yet?"

Luke nodded, swallowed hard, and said he would certainly give the matter his attention, making a mental note to have a cable ship on the ledgers very quickly. It was the first time Luke had heard of the ship, but whatever — a ship today, a lipstick factory tomorrow. Anything to keep Geneen happy.

Things moved fast after that. Luke found where the ship request was hung up in the chain of command. He cleared it for action. A hurried request for negotiations was made of the surprised owners, who were delighted at the prospect of selling what they regarded as a white elephant. With no cable-laying business the ship had rusted on its own coffee grounds in the Philippines for two years on a meager air force contract, insufficient to support itself or the Hollywood casting studio offices of the U.S. Underseas Cable Corporation in Washington.

Haggling might have held up the deal, but at each impasse Geneen said buy, and negotiations quickly resumed. Luke sweated, cursed, moaned that the company was being had — but talked on.

On questioning the ITT principals in the action Luke learned that no one from ITT had seen the ship recently. A marine consultant was dispatched in haste to the Philippines to be sure the ship was physically there. The voluminous report he submitted two weeks later was scanned quickly and tossed aside. The consultant had done a thorough job of detailing the hundreds of discrepancies he had noted in his inspection — but nothing was read by Luke after the fact was confirmed that such a ship did exist.

George Banino's reaction was predictable: disgust.

"What the hell is on your shopping list of tomorrow, the Empire State Building?" He croaked a wicked laugh. "I remember the last guy we hired who wanted to buy a cable ship. Some retired air force colonel. He wrote Geneen a proposal and they set him up in a Washington suite. Plushiest office I've ever seen — it looked like the Joint Chiefs of Staff War Room. Clocks all over the walls for the world time zones. Sliding glass walls with maps on them. Cable ship models that must have cost ten grand apiece. Everything, the whole schmeer. He lasted until the next Business Plan Meeting. It cost us about fifty grand to cancel his lease and pay him off. And we never did buy him the goddam ship. So good luck."

But if Banino didn't agree with our desire to own a ship there were others who accepted the procurement assignment with enthusiasm. Ships were fun to buy. ITT lawyers had a great time researching this new area. Luke's buying team enjoyed the Washington stay.

Only the accountants seemed unhappy. Negotiations went on for the cable communications equipment that U.S.U.C.C. had stashed in dark cellars in Germany. The rights to cable guard programs that involved the dubious privilege of landing in Russia were snapped up. As the negotiations moved along in a lighthearted atmosphere the unleashed purchasing power of ITT was more and more impressive. The ITT negotiators seemed to be under the impression that they were buying a special bauble for Geneen, personally, and wanted to be sure all of the extras were included. Buying plumbing supply manufacturers could be a drag, but buying cable ships was a sort of comic relief. So the ITT negotiators bought on — anything of value U.S.U.C.C. could dredge up. The ship owners scoured their junk piles for "extras" to inflate the purchase.

On learning of Geneen's interest, everyone wanted to be in on the act. The navy was contacted by the ITT Washington Office and grandiose projections for the use of the ship were developed. The air force was also tapped and responded with interest. Dita Beard in a parallel effort conducted a "Name the Ship" contest. The winning entry was *The San Diego Queen*, submitted, naturally, by a member of Congressman Wilson's staff. Tom Casey offered to arrange to rent the ship outright to the chief of navy materiel for ten years to "generate some cash flow." The idea had a lot of appeal until it was explained that if the navy rented it for their programs full time it was of no use to ITT. Casey withdrew his generous offer reluctantly.

After weeks of midnight-oil burning, negotiations were completed and we departed — leaving the formal signing to Stan Luke's crew of legal specialists. Luke called from New York a few days later in a sour mood. We talked on a three-way conference call, Washington, New York, and San Diego.

"We bought your goddam ship," he said. "Make arrangements to pick it up in Washington. From now on it's your baby. Understand?"

"Right Stan, we understand. Thank you for buying the ship."

"That's O.K. Next time give me a little more time, will you?" he said. "What are you guys looking to buy next time?"

"A zeppelin," I said. I laughed. Luke hung up. "He didn't think it was funny," said the staff consultant, and he hung up too.

It was a mere detail that the ship's blueprints were in Washington and the ship was in Subic Bay in the Philippines. We were grateful to Luke for a magnificent buy, well executed with vigor and determination.

The following week at the plush but now almost vacant
offices of the U.S. Underseas Cable Corporation in Washington, we presented ourselves to pick up the *Neptun* blueprints, records and plans. Workmen were removing an
exotic collection of world globes, cable ship pictures and
magnificent antique furniture from the suite. The "good
will" exchange took place in a frigid, formal atmosphere.
We had, after all, bought the company and were putting
these remaining executives out to pasture. The meeting had
all the joviality of the Japanese surrender aboard the *Mis-
souri*. The brief and sometimes painful formalities completed, we walked down the office corridors to the entrance
foyer. Next to the president's suite was a model of the
Neptun, under glass, three feet long and in fine detail.

"Can we arrange to have this shipped to San Diego?" I
asked the U.S.U.C.C. president.

Drawing himself to his full five-foot five-inch height and
sucking in his ample paunch, he replied with disdain, "You
may have bought the cable ship and our equipment, but
nothing was said about this model. The model stays. It's not
for sale."

The miracle ITT buying machine that had closed the
complex ship acquisition in three weeks had been bilked
out of what I thought might eventually prove to be the most
valuable part of the whole deal. Gift-wrapped, the model
would have made a great birthday present for Geneen. The
Neptun was, after all, just another piece of gear for the
hired help to make work. The model, on the other hand,
was a handsome toy, painted all of those bright red and
yellow colors that Geneen enjoyed so much.

Abbott

FEW THINGS WE DID at the Cable Division were more unpleasant than dealing with Joe Abbott — very few. Joe had been the Defense Space Group's public relations director since the beginning of time. He was a tall, rather dull, pompous egocentric — who, if crossed, was very dangerous. He could do very little to help the division, but a great deal to lay the wood to us managers in the highest ITT circles if he were so disposed.

Abbott had written me long lays and cantos concerning the need to appoint an advertising agency to handle the division's program. But we wanted no program, we had no products which needed pizzazz and no desire to part with the money for such services. So we stalled. To end our modest protestations Abbott had an ultimatum issued from New York. We were to sign up a local agency. Abbott announced a visit to check on our compliance.

So our holdout was at an end, alas. But if we could find the money to beef up the budget, what the hell. Why not

have some advertising people hanging around. Abbott's
case was made before he boarded the plane in New York.
But rather than spoil his fun I let him come to San Diego
to beat us into line personally. The meeting was scheduled
for two, but Joe arrived huffing and puffing at three at our
downtown offices with Norm Tolle in tow. Tolle was president of the San Diego advertising agency closely tied to
Congressman Bob Wilson. We were not surprised at Tolle's
covert selection by New York. He had worked for Abbott
over the years on special assignments and secret missions. If
the purpose of the meeting was to counsel me with respect
to the selection of the San Diego advertising agency, Tolle's
presence made it a total waste of time. Although the choice
was mine, unfortunately for Abbott, the clout was with
him and it should have been obvious I had decided to live
to fight another day by avoiding his wrath. I had turned
down one of his unemployed friends only a week before as
a candidate for division advertising manager in my marketing organization. It would be the second strike if I sent
Tolle away empty-handed. So with rape inevitable, I relaxed and greeted the odd couple cordially. Unfortunately
Joe was intent and businesslike; he was expecting to hard-
sell me after all. With Abbott so disposed it could be a long
afternoon.

Together, Tolle and Abbott were a striking pair. Both
were balding with a gray fringe. Abbott was ponderous and
looked very much like a walrus. Tolle was slight and looked
like a seal. The pair together looked like an advertisement
for *Sea World*.

For some obscure reason, Abbott was a professional

Notre Dame man. I could never understand why he vindic-
tively waved a Fighting Irish banner in my face at every
opportunity. He told the same Notre Dame stories over and
over. I had suffered before through an obscure Notre Dame
track team's glories as the team of the century at least a
dozen times. And the football sagas lasted for hours. Abbott was also an old-school politician brought up in the
"knuckle and skull" New Jersey period when Frank Hague
was supervising all the ex-choirboys turned ward bosses.
At this he was very skilled — but told no stories of the old
days. Joe was animal-shrewd and tough. He bumbled, stut-
tered, was fat all over, and sometimes acted the fool. But he
was a man to be respected; the battlefields of ITT were
strewn with the bleaching bones of people who had
laughed at Abbott's appearance and discounted his influence.

Since any substantial advertising campaign for the division was months away, my decision to capitulate and let
Abbott sign the Tolle Agency to a contract was no big deal.
Our major sales efforts were six months away; fortunes
would change greatly in that time. Reputation-wise, Tolle
was among the first five seeded in San Diego. And a San
Diego ad agency would be allowed to handle only the bits
and pieces anyway; any major campaign would be
mounted by the ITT corporate advertising staff in New
York — further minimizing the impact of my decision.
Public relations and advertising were not decentralized in
ITT; all direction came from Vice President Gerrity
through the Mecca tieline. The more I thought about it the
less difference it made to me who got the agency contract.

But to Joe it was another matter; his pride was at stake, and he wanted to throw some of his substantial weight around.

"Well, Tom, you know Norm here, I guess," Abbott said. "You know Bob Wilson is on Tolle's payroll. He's a partner of Norm's."

Right out on the table. Good boy, Joe.

Tolle waved Joe off. I thought he might bark like a seal. "No, no, that's not quite true anymore, Joe. Bob is a vice president of the company, but he is only marginally associated with us. I wouldn't want his name brought into our discussions."

Joe waved Tolle off. "Sure. Sure. We know how it is. Anyway, these Tolle people are friends of Wilson, and a lot of the other people we do business with in San Diego. Know what I mean?"

"Sure, Joe," I said. "I get the point. Nice to be among friends."

"Right," Joe said. "Right. Stay with people you know. Have you looked at any other ad agencies? Any local ones, I mean?"

I had sent him detailed reports on four other San Diego agencies. Perhaps he didn't read his mail. Or perhaps he knew I was pulling his leg and ignored my glowing praise for Tolle competitors.

"Yeah, Joe. I've looked at a few others. Had a few short presentations, just to get an idea of who's available."

"Some very good advertising people have moved down from Los Angeles," Tolle said. "We're proud of our advertising community here."

Maybe it would not be necessary to go through the entire

mating dance with feathers flying, hopping on one flat claw. At the first opportunity I would warmly agree and have it over. But Abbott was not giving me that opportunity. He would have his pound of flesh.

"Norm would give you a presentation, but you can take my word for it, his stuff is good. We've used it for years," Abbott said.

From the advertising grapevine I'd heard that Tolle and his lieutenants had let it be known weeks ago that our account was in their pocket. Since Joe wouldn't get to the point I was tempted to play hard to get. But there was a chance that would just prolong the farce. So I tried to capitulate in a hurry.

"No question about it, Joe. As I understand the situation, you are recommending Tolle Agency as being probably our wisest choice. That being the case, I must be guided by your experience in these matters. If Norm has brought along a contract, maybe we could look it over and initial it and ship it back to our public relations and legal people in New York." I smiled winningly and reached for my silver Parker.

Surprise swept slowly over Joe's face. He sputtered. I had fallen too easily. Joe had been expecting a recalcitrant whippersnapper, someone who was going to buck his system. He was prepared to twist an arm a little and put the kid in his place.

"You know, it's your choice. I can't tell you who to select," he said, his voice heavy with suspicion.

Tolle was confused. Things were not proceeding as planned. I acted all pro and now Joe was acting some con.

"Yes, I realize that. And, as I said, I've talked to a few other agencies. But you tell me that Norm is well connected and he knows all our people, and that he and Congressman Wilson —"

Joe banged his fist on the table. "We can't let considerations like that sway us in these matters." He looked hard at Tolle. "Norm, you wouldn't expect us to make a decision on any basis like that, would you?"

Poor old Tolle thought he was being sandbagged. He started to speak but Joe boomed over him, "Goddam right, you wouldn't." Joe turned to me. "But there are some things that we have to consider. You know that Norm has been a friend of Mr. Geneen's for a long time. He's done some very fine work for him; haven't you, Norm?"

Tolle nodded, now completely confused. He reached for his briefcase and I expected him to bolt and run.

"Show him some pictures, Norm." There was happy Harold Sydney Geneen smiling up at me from two dozen cheerful photographs.

"That's good enough for me," I said. "Any friend of —"

"Just a minute, Tom," Abbott said. "We can't make any positive commitment today, of course. I mean, I really should check up with Gerrity before we do anything final. I mean, you know Gerrity is taking a personal interest in this San Diego thing. Since we've made some commitments —"

"Great," I said. "As soon as Gerrity gives his O.K. I think we might initial the contract and get this arrangement under way."

"There are going to be some big doings here that you

don't know about," Abbott said in a wise old bird croak, "and I mean big doings. And you division guys are going to need all the help that you can get from some good public relations people like Norm here. Know what I mean?"

"No, Joe, I don't. But that's all right, there's no reason that I should. We'll play them as they lie." Joe rocked back in his chair, and I remembered old cartoons of Boss Tweed. Tolle wanted to be off before the ITT confidences began to be swapped. He wanted no part of an Abbott "*entre nous*" session.

"Norm, why don't you leave your rate schedule and a contract and I'll take it from there," I said, helping him out.

Tolle quickly brought forth the previously prepared document from his bag. He now wanted the meeting over as much as I did. If Abbott warmed up to the situation any further we could be in for hours of conversation, confidences, and convictions neither of us wanted to be exposed to.

"So, it will be your decision. I hope you make the right one," Joe rattled on. I noticed he was addressing his reflection in the windows across the room.

"Well, it was difficult. As Norm said, there is a lot of outstanding advertising talent in this area. But, there you are, we can only choose one, and I think Norm and I can get together."

Tolle was on his feet, shaking hands. "Thank you very much. Call us any time. Our account manager will drop in this week."

"It is your decision and I hope you make a wise one," Abbott said, hypnotized by his reflection and still in the future tense. Tolle and I headed for the conference room door at a fast pace. Unless the light changed quickly we could leave Joe to his reverie and save the better part of a working afternoon.

Or Else

"You can't expect anything from Ma Bell, Western Electric, or the Navy CAESAR Office," Valente, now a senior V.P., repeated as the cab passed the Lincoln Monument and headed for the Memorial Bridge. "You've just got to understand you don't have any friends. The whole thing has to be done by brute force, and my reputation and your reputations are all on the line, in spades, and don't forget it for a moment."

He confuses employment with reputation, I thought.

The ocean engineering manager looked grim. He was an ex-Western Electric man and a recent hire. I hoped he would hold his temper; we only had a mile or so to Valente's drop at the Sheraton.

"You guys have put twenty million into the ground already," Valente went on, "and I don't see any end in sight. Somehow we've got to make these forecasts jell, if you know what I mean — and pretty goddam soon. Commitments are what we need — contracts, promises. Give me a full, detailed report next week. Rich Bennett will be on my ass until I can tell him something specific. This is serious, goddam serious."

The cab stopped at a swinging bar a block from the Sheraton.

"A complete report, don't forget," said Valente as he jumped out. The engineer and I rode on to the Mayflower.

"I don't like dealing with desperate people," the engineer said. "That son-of-a-bitch is frightened. Is this a typical ITT reaction?"

I nodded but decided against telling him any more. Why be discouraging; he'd find out for himself soon enough.

Memo Come Back to Me...

THE PRODUCT LINE MANAGER was frightened. And not without reason. His secretary, a comely blonde Amazon who weighed a well-proportioned 200 pounds, was waved out on a chase as we entered the office.

"Find it!" the manager shouted after her. "The goddam cable market study said 'monopoly' in one place, a projection. Not a fact, an estimate. My boss read it and went into shock. He has three people out on the floor gathering it up, all the copies. One goddam word, in a personal and confidential memorandum."

"Cable monopoly?" I said. "Where the hell can you claim a cable monopoly?"

He waved his hand. "It was just describing a situation that could come about. *Could* — a figure of speech, nothing important. Just a description to juice up a little support from the goddam staff. What else do you call a situation that is a monopoly?"

"Cosa Nostra, Bank of Japan, Politburo —"

"Sure. Or 'Tea for Two.' But why do we have to mince our words when we are talking to each other?"

"Are you getting soft?" the British cable engineer asked. "We don't have all your problems with semantics in Europe. We call them as they finish, you know. Cartels, agreements —"

The product line manager glared at him, exasperated. "Europe is Europe," he told him. "In this country we have some small problems with words like 'monopoly.' It was stupid, I should have used a couple of four-letter words for effect instead. And if they don't stop the circulation before the copies reach Bennett or Geneen, I'll be looking for a job."

"Come to Europe," the engineer said. "You can use whatever words you bloody well like."

Take the Money and Run

VALENTE'S REPLACEMENT as Defense Space Group vice president had called the meeting at Nutley. Around the table sat twelve representatives of his legal, public relations, and operations staffs. Our three-man contingent was positioned at the end of the table, reports piled in front of us as a defense against the mini-inquisition.

Finally, after a ten-minute wait, the new group vice president, Rand Araskog, entered flanked by George Banino and Bob Chasen, our "executive coordinator." He was tall, thin, and looked awed at this first confrontation in an unfamiliar area of the defense business.

We had speculated on what he had been told concerning our money problems. We concluded not much beyond the bare investment figures, which were frightening enough. The cable project was at a crucial point, an additional $5 million was needed immediately with perhaps $5 million more later in the month. Alas, all over budget.

Araskog had heard of our Washington contract wars and San Diego construction problems. I guessed he was concerned over the Pentagon repercussions that were certain to follow whatever decisions were made at this meeting. "No" to the additional investment meant a Pentagon problem; "yes" was an ITT treasurer's problem. Alas for poor Rand.

Araskog was a West Pointer who probably should have stayed in uniform instead of becoming a Smoke Rise squire, country club type, an ersatz organization man. He tried to do the whole bit, but wound up a martinet, junior class. Now he had a promotion to bigger problems and more agonizing decisions.

How could we hope to be understood by such a timid congregation? I thought of Geneen's bombasts that in such directions lies perpetual mediocrity. Before the meeting began I saw the signposts pointing out some very timid directions, indeed. And our general manager was a match for the caution of the assembled staffs to make our case a sure loss before we began. Together they all agreed $5 million was a lot of money and would, I felt, try hard to bump the decision to a higher level.

The meeting lasted barely fifteen minutes. It was obvious the investment figures frightened Araskog. No one had any questions. The reports submitted were incomplete, Araskog said, the potential losses from adverse operations were too staggering for him to pass on. Someone up the line had to make this decision, he pleaded. The staff in unison nodded agreement. Not him. Not today, certainly. We stood in amazement as he apologized, turning gradually a pasty green and in appearance physically ill, and excused himself. Banino shook his head sadly and adjourned the meeting.

"That's the first intelligent reaction I've seen to the handling of this program," I said. "Araskog went out and puked. But it doesn't help much."

Our controller nodded. "I guess he has a queasy stomach. Maybe gradually he'll get used to all this. After all, someone has to face up to it."

Only the group's Dr. Strangelove, a sinister Austrian engineering consultant, stopped by to wish us well in a Viennese-laced Jersey idiom. He volunteered us the use of his reputation and six-doctorate pedigree with the military establishment, if we were in need of such support. Peter Lorre to the rescue, I thought.

Next day at lunch at the Capitol Hill Club, I described the meeting to Dita Beard. She listened without surprise, the problems of non-support from ITT top management an old story to her.

"Man for man," Dita observed, "there are more paper ass-holes in ITT than any organization in the world. Screw those pansies in Nutley. Just be sure your story gets to Geneen; you'll get the money. How do you think I've survived all these years?"

The Stockholders' Meeting

WE HAD BEEN through the ITT Stockholders' Meeting and Board of Directors' Meeting in San Diego. This three-week ordeal involved arranging visits to the cable plant site in National City and preparing presentations for the North American staff on the future of the cable manufacturing complex. The staff, in turn, presented our gaudy slides and spellbinding story to the board with monologue by Maurie Valente and side comments by Rich Bennett. Our engineers even made expensive models of factories that might never be. But most of all we made sure the logistics were provided for meetings between Geneen, Wilson, and a host of other ITT and local San Diego personalities, famous and infamous. To help out our infant Cable Division public relations effort New York assigned a team of advertising professionals, and we had a lot of volunteer support from the local press and convention bureau. But we were far out of our league in trying to arrange the kind of activities a major stockholders' meeting involves. Finally the ITT New

York advertising and PR pros simply took over and we lent a helping hand on request. And somehow, everything came off on schedule. Activity and confusion peaked on the final day of the Stockholders' Meeting. But we persevered in the knowledge that with one more round of merriment, the division would be rid of the whole ITT entourage and their local camp followers.

The farewell cocktail party was held at one of the smaller ballrooms at C. Arnholdt Smith's opulent Westgate Plaza Hotel. Geneen was at a door to greet honored guests, flanked by San Diego's financial and social community, the ITT board of directors, a dozen senior vice presidents, and, of course, Dita Beard. Norm Tolle's advertising people took pictures from all angles, the executives striking imposing poses and Dita adjusting their ties. Members of the corporate and Washington staffs stationed themselves around the room to provide conversation points. The buffet and bar were like all ITT senior management productions — the last word in catering and libation; it was an atmosphere heavy with shop talk, serious boozing, and boss buttering.

Rumors had been circulating all week about a meeting between Geneen and Wilson, to make final arrangements for the ITT contribution for the Republican Convention. The contribution included ITT staff public relations support, ITT Sheraton hotel services, cash money direct, check money indirect, and a number of other helpful and lucrative assists. Geneen was sure Nixon was the one for four more years and was prepared to demonstrate his confidence with good works. The convention issue had been kicking around San Diego for a long time without achieving much

local support. There were many Southern California politicians who wanted to bask in the reflected glory of such an
event. But there were the other San Diego people with a big
say — hotel operators, city officials, and most of the business community — who were concerned about the financial drain on the city and the problem of riots. Convention
time was vacation time — and San Diego had plenty of
tourist trade without adding a hoard of brown-bagging
rowdy Republicans to tax the always overcrowded accommodations.

"Anyone who thinks that they can hold a national political convention in the San Diego Sports Arena simply
doesn't know anything about conventions," one of the ITT
public relations managers said. "Geneen says he wants the
convention here, for whatever reasons. O.K. He is trying to
do something nice for Wilson. And Nixon. Again, O.K. But
if the convention has to be held here, we need some advance
notice. You can be sure that Geneen will want the ITT
troops here en masse. We will probably wind up running
the whole goddam affair. So the earlier we get the go-ahead
the easier it will be for everyone concerned."

"But our illustrious mayor, Frank Curran, of taxicab
fame, doesn't want the convention. And the city business
community doesn't want the convention. And most of the
hotel people don't want the convention," a newspaper
editor said, "so who the hell besides Geneen is pushing for
a convention in San Diego?"

"The White House," the ITT public relations manager
said. "Geneen, Nixon, Wilson, and the Republican followers of that troupe."

"Not a bad one-two to try to make happy in an election year; Congressman Bob, who controls the heavy contributions for the party; and Tricky Dicky, who looks like a shoo-in for re-election. If I were Geneen, I'd certainly be inclined to be rather generous," said a real estate man.

All too true. We knew by way of Dita Beard and Wilson's staff that Bob Wilson had long since received an assurance from Geneen that ITT would spring for whatever was needed to match local contributions. The figure quoted was up to $600 thousand, but the ITT staff people said that no reasonable figure would be beyond Geneen's pocketbook. Six hundred thousand, one million, or whatever — so long as the thing was done discreetly. The meeting in San Diego would iron out the details of when and how the pledges were to be delivered.

The party clamor rose as the hours passed and the sun slid further over the yardarm.

Rich Bennett was really high. He came over and threw his arms around me, pounded my back, and congratulated me for the great job we had done with the arrangements for the Stockholders' Meeting. Since our division people had acted as third-hand, unskilled help to the ITT New York public relations corps, I took the compliment with the modesty it deserved.

"Now we're gonna have the Republican Convention here," Rich said. "You have a chance to really show that Cable Division off. It cost us a bundle — Christ, $25 million in the ground already. But it was worth it. Sure as hell was worth it, the way things are going."

After some reminiscences about the old early days when

the Cable Division project was just a gleam in his eye, Rich pumped my hand and with a tear of gratitude congratulated me again on the job well done and smartly under way. He wandered off and was lost to a host of admirers. I was shortly accosted by all the senior managers within view and earshot for a sampling of the super chief's remarks and sentiments.

"He asked me where the best piece of ass in San Diego was hiding out," I lied. They got the point and drifted off.

"These locals are going to back off their half-million-dollar commitment as fast as they can as soon as ITT starts pouring money in," an ITT advertising man said. "We've been assigned to work with the Civic Host Committee and the hotel owners and the Convention and Visitors' Bureau. And believe me, none of them are moving very fast. The San Diego contributions are just a trickle so far. Mark my words, this is going to be an ITT-sponsored party, and if this guy Graham is smart, he'll hold out until Geneen buys the Sports Arena."

The strange thing about the convention conversation was that there was no unanimity about what the Grand Old Party wanted the city to come up with for a package offer. Among the leaders of the important Republican factions, different stories were being circulated. They were singing off the Republican song sheets, but without harmony.

Bob Wilson was being accused of trying to fly the whole convention solo, without consulting the long established and firmly entrenched Republican establishment in San Diego. And these long-in-tooth crusty old characters would have none of his direction.

"This is a play on Wilson's part to set up a power base here," a city official with strong ties to the mayor said. "We think that he's trying to set himself up to run for governor, with Nixon's support, in 1974. He isn't asking for Curran's support, and he isn't asking for Smith's support; and he's going to be goddam sorry in the end that he didn't."

Mayor Frank Curran was the creation of financier C. Arnholdt Smith and, according to local political pundits, might be ignored since his loyalty as a nominal Democrat was in question. But to exclude Smith from the convention considerations and deliberations was unthinkable. No one seemed to be quite sure why the local Republican money bags had been snubbed. Wilson may have felt he was ready for a shot at the top spot in California, with a little favorable publicity and the support of Nixon politically and of Geneen financially. But even so, why freeze Smith and the local bankers — unless Wilson was privy to some most sensitive IRS secret information concerning the financial manipulations within the Westgate California cartel which Smith controlled. The scrolls of intrigue were too deep for most of the party faithful to decipher. Republicans simply chose up sides and waited for someone to play power politics and move the convention issue.

Alarms, rumors, and diversions continued to circulate, but only one conclusion was logical. Certainly Wilson had the credits in the right places to bid for the governorship, or even to make it a race for the Senate seat when Alan Cranston came up for reelection in 1974. The Wilson alternate to the parochial support of the California Republican king-makers was to establish ties to the White House and build his war chest through people like Geneen. Then Wilson would be in full command. He refused to dangle until Smith and his cohorts decided his fate. Not with friends like Nixon and Geneen ready to support him.

Our operations vice president was talking with a black man decked out in a conservative purple suit and beige high-button shoes. He introduced himself as the duty black, representative of the NAACP, and an executive of a county poverty program.

"I like to be invited to these things, no matter who sponsors them," he said, "you know — to see how the other half lives. Grist for the mill. You pick up more information at a party like this than reading the *San Diego Union* for a year."

The duty black man drifted off toward the bar. "He was sweating me about employment at the plants," our operations man said. "We're never going to convince anyone that four hundred people is about all we are going to need, forever, unless New York decides to put up two or three more plants and can find a spare sixty or eighty million dollars to do it."

"Recent studies indicate the payoff for such a program is about two thousand years, with luck," I said. "I can see Geneen supporting a convention or two, but I can't see him supporting a first-class financial disaster."

The operations man laughed. "That son-of-a-bitch, Geneen — we tried for two days to make arrangements to have him tour the cable plant. Every other bigwig passed through at one time or another. Then yesterday, I get back from this Westgate Plaza circus; and the superintendent

tells me that Geneen dropped in all by himself. Brought the
security guard from the gate along and the three of them
walked through the plant. My troops on standby for a
week, and he has a chatty little visit with the construction
superintendent and security guard. Told them he asked his
wife to come along, but she decided to go shopping in
Tijuana instead."

"Well, you better batten down for more of the same," I
said. "Dita's racing around the social circuit scattering invitations to future ITT parties and our public relations
boys are sizing things up — I think the Republican National Convention is in the bag for San Diego and we are
the hosts."

"You mean San Diego is the host city?"

"I mean that ITT is the financial supporter; and if I can
believe these advertising types, the whole thing will be
wrapped up at a friendly dinner tonight. We are the angels
of the convention, according to Dita. You'd better trade in
that threadbare tuxedo on something more appropriate for
the entertainment committee."

"The committee I could handle," he said. "I'm more concerned about Jerry Rubin leading a hippy parade of nudes
on our beach front. That would be trouble."

The Wildeboar Chronicles

WE WAITED in the Los Angeles International Airport to claim the remains of W. L. P. Wildeboar. The recently retired engineering executive of ITT Standard Telephone Cables in the United Kingdom was winging in from London via Pan American 747. The long polar trip, in popular opinion, Wildeboar would not survive, since it was eighteen hours of limitless liquor and first-class attention. The combination of temptation and opportunity was expected to render comatose, moribund, and finally demised the gallant Sir Wildeboar, of the gentle heart and noble thirst.

We positioned ourselves on the balcony above the Pan Am arrival rotunda, relaying drinks from the Clipper Club and keeping a sharp watch. We had been impressed by Wildeboar's countrymen with the responsibility of our vigil. If we missed Wildeboar and he wandered off into the Los Angeles night it might be a long time before he was discovered. A pub-to-pub man of jovial and friendly manner, he could circulate for days in and among the watering holes and libation dispensaries of the City of the Angels.

When all of the London passengers had left and there was still no sign of a visitor matching his tweedy, mustached, bespectacled description we became mildly alarmed. Our concern mounted as we could get no response from buttonholing Pan American officials. His description was shrugged off, his presence denied. Finally a porter, one of the last to leave, motioned back of the loading platform. There was W. L. P., sitting, smiling, apparently chatting with a gum-vending machine. He was sodden, his clothes disheveled, in worse shape than predicted. After an eighteen-hour carouse, his general area smelled as though a hand grenade had gone off in a liquor cabinet. He seemed to be shrunk to almost midget size, the picture of a gentleman in his humors, slightly jostled.

We fortified Lee with a few quick belts and hustled him away to the Disneyland Hotel for an overnight stay. Our directions were to transport him in short hops to San Diego, with no extended cold-turkey periods, until he became adjusted. The Mickey Mouse Kingdom was to be our first oasis stop along the way.

As we rolled onto the San Diego Freeway he came to life. Wildeboar recounted in page, verse, and round the saga of his transpolar flight, including the attention of each and every comely stewardess with a description from curve of hip to point of breast.

"Many years since I've set foot here, you know," he said. "Nice to be back in the colonies. I don't suppose things have changed much?"

No, we assured him. Nothing had changed in ten years. California now had indoor plumbing, color television, and even a few bars that served cocktails after midnight.

We checked him in at the Disneyland Hotel and were persuaded to adjourn to the cocktail lounge for a nightcap. As we hauled Wildeboar through the swinging doors he stumbled, and I was sure he had packed it in. But no, we realized that the dark cocktail lounge had merely scrambled his rods and cones. What a gallon of Scotch had not done, the low red lighting of the cocktail lounge managed — Wildeboar staggered.

"Damn, whoever heard of lighting a pub with fireflies," he said. "I can't see a damn thing. How do you know what you're drinking? Bloody stupid, drinking in the dark."

Wildeboar looked like a mysterious gnome perched at the bar. A sinister sleepwalker with a cigarette dangling from the side of his mouth, glowing brightly in time with his barking cough. Wildeboar of Transylvania in the Land of Snow White. The strain was beginning to tell and we tried for a quick exit. But no, he began planning an extensive Disneyland tour.

"Here's where I'd like to go."

He wrote on his napkin a list which he read to us for comment; Mickey Mouse's House, Cave Full of Dwarves, Donald Duck's Uncle, and The Mechanical Lincoln were included. We begged off as guides, orienting him with respect to the monorail at his doorstep which would whisk him into the park in a few minutes. We redrafted his list to include some of the more appropriate attractions — including Toad's Wild Ride and the Mad Hatter's Tea Party.

We neglected to mention that there was not a pub within the confines of Disneyland, lest Wildeboar decide to carry something on the hip and be rousted by the park police. Finally, we managed to file Wildeboar away, sure that total exhaustion would keep him away from all spirits, evil and otherwise, until morning.

"Pickup time at lunch, Lee old man, don't be late. Goodnight."

The times I'd done business with Wildeboar in England he impressed me as a brisk, no-nonsense engineering administrator. It was from Hayden Moore that I heard of his reputation as the bon vivant of the European cable industry. Moore had traveled on continental junkets with him, attending telecommunications conferences. Wildeboar was an acknowledged expert in plastic extrusion technology and invited to most of the electrical engineering boondoggles as a featured speaker. For all of his merrymaking and eccentricities, Lee Wildeboar was regarded as a sound technical man of international reputation, just what the fledgling Cable Division needed to put the seal of approval on our market research reports and assorted daydreams.

Unknown to Wildeboar, his mission was also of utmost importance to the ITT North American staff and the Defense Space Group management. Responsible for our fortunes, our top management were worried about Geneen's urging that we busy ourselves planning a telephone cable plant at San Diego. Congressman Wilson was pressing for our second factory and the thousand jobs he imagined went with it. Geneen suggested that a foundation hole be put in the ground and construction started — but only if our management would bless the project as at least a nominally profitable venture. Alas, there was the rub.

Rumblings came back from the spies we maintained close to the throne that Rich Bennett was being harassed by Geneen to push ahead. So studies were undertaken as a first step, employing a small army of ITT market research and product planning groups from New York, Nutley, and Brussels. The Cable Division had been commissioned to conduct our own homemade, independent effort — a folksy little backup study. But soon the North American Staff became distraught and confused, caught as they were between Bennett's pressure and their reluctance to support a project they felt had no chance of success. They turned more and more to the Cable Division marketeers for help. And more and more often they even said it: "HELP!" Hard crow for proud staff men to eat at a humble division table.

"Bennett is a poker player par excellence," a staff man confided. "We have been through this before. When one of his projects is in trouble, he tries to raise the ante. He is telling Geneen that we will get big chunks of telephone business as a settlement for the suit against General Telephone. But we are telling him that even if we did, it would have to go out the door at competitive prices, and that is where the San Diego project falls flat on its ass. The plant on the drawing board will never compete. But he doesn't tell Geneen such unpleasant facts. Why, we don't know. And of course we don't ask. So Geneen keeps prodding and Bennett keeps pushing."

Confidential memoranda flew like a paper blizzard.

SYOA (Save Your Own Ass) documents for the most part, reservations in writing to have ready when the inquisition began. Whether the number or the logic of these uncirculated staff reports finally impressed the Defense Space Group management, we weren't sure. But they reluctantly came to the decision to kill the cable plant project, even at the risk of leaving Bennett out on a limb. Obviously, without Bennett's support, the little murder of the project was a great risk and had to be done with utmost discretion. But with the first factory, the submarine cable manufacturing facility already racing ahead of the budget projections, and the news from AT&T disclosing a depressing sales picture, the group management could see no profit soon or late. They would budge no further down the primrose path of additional capital investment. Plant two, the telephone cable manufacturing facility, was never to be. Neither were plants three or four, or more.

I had assigned the division market research department to pore over the studies made by and for ITT market researchers over the years. Planning the entry of ITT into telecommunications cable business seemed to be a favorite way to plug up spare staff time. The information accumulated over the years was voluminous, making up in sheer bulk what it lacked in quality. The most recent addition to the long record was a report prepared by a consulting team from Arthur D. Little, the prestigious Boston management consultant. It was a year old and summarized the data previously compiled by the swarms of ITT researchers and new facts discovered by the A. D. Little team. Sensing what ITT management wanted to hear, A. D. L. interpreted their findings to show some chance for success for ITT in the telecommunications cable business — somewhere, somehow, sometime. But professional as they were, they were forced to trade popularity and the possibility of follow-on contracts for truth. The faint praise of such a project was what A. D. L. researchers ruefully but bravely put forth to squelch the project. Reading between the lines the A. D. L. report said, "ITT, you had better forget the whole thing."

But somehow the underlying message was ignored — and now forgotten. Here we were a year later rousing ourselves for an onslaught on the entrenched competition of AT&T and GTE, only this time the report was not to be made by a consultant with an objective point of view. The report would be made by ITT's very own experts in New York and San Diego, and no one involved was naive enough to think that the results would be viewed kindly by Geneen if they suggested the San Diego factory building high adventure spree was kaput. But how to say "maybe go ahead," and really mean "stop," and get out from under on that Judgment Day when the profit numbers rolled in — that was the staff's dilemma.

No one was anxious to burst a Geneen bubble and incur the wrath of a couple of executive vice presidents. But on the other hand the responsibility for a big, long-term financial disaster was suicide. With the potential of one such disaster nearing completion in San Diego a second would have been silly for the managers to support, the equivalent of making razorblade sandwiches. Skill, cunning, and guile à la ITT were called for, but the project must die aborning. They wept bitterly over the necessity of opposing Bennett, no matter how well they might be concealed behind a mountain of reports and data, but they knew it was inevitable to the continuity of their employment. So they joined in a group sabotage plot.

"At some point this bullshit has to end," the group vice president said. "The group's rationale is that a gentle, slightly negative report will be enough to turn things off for a while. The telecommunications cable program runs out of support slowly on all levels. All the way to the top. And Geneen finally admits the time is not ripe. But when us chickens start dancing with those elephants a lot of feathers will be flying. What a lousy position you San Diego bastards have put all of us in."

So group management discovered and signed up Wildeboar — they would have had to invent him if he hadn't existed — as a homegrown ITT European telephone cable expert who would tell it like it was. We were assured Wildeboar was so negative on investment in the colonies he would price any cable project out of sight. And all the ITT experts would then agree — in short, the ideal fall-back position for the group managers.

The morning visit to Disneyland was a tonic to Wildeboar after his long, wet flight. At lunch he looked bright and dapper with a fresh tweed outfit and green bow tie. No trace of the devastating hangover or shaky hand that one might have expected. He talked endlessly about his Disneyland frolic and was delighted by the rolling miles of flower gardens, groves, and seascapes of the San Diego Freeway. He recognized Capistrano, "where the swallows return to," and San Clemente, "where Nixon stays when he visits." We stopped to rubberneck the atomic energy generating plant at San Onofre. He waved at drivers as we passed, something I took to be a Welsh custom, but a questionable distraction at eighty-mile-per-hour speeds. Truck drivers registered some surprise, but most people grinned and waved back. A Volkswagen filled with bikini-clad teenagers mimed and made some gestures it was just as well Lee didn't comprehend. But all in all, he seemed delighted at being under California skies and at the prospect of beginning his first consulting assignment.

At the division headquarters office we turned him over to the Florence Nightingale instincts of the secretarial corps. These ladies were skilled in the nuturing of consultants, displaced managers, soldiers of fortune, and stray cats. We knew that Wildeboar would be well cared for and maneuvered through such complexities of office routine as where he could buy a Coke and how to make his way to the men's room.

The controller stood by watching these miniskirted ambassadors of hospitality leading Wildeboar around and arranging his office. "If that son-of-a-bitch can function he'll have them all laid in a week," he said.

"I don't know about his prowess," Moore said, "but he was the only man I knew who could act as a committee chairman at a technical conference without leaving the lobby bar."

"Well, just so long as you and he wind up singing off the same sheet of music. He brought his rubber stamp along, I trust," the controller said. "Tell him if he kills our telephone cable caper I'll be rather lenient with his expense account."

The following day our market research team piled Wildeboar's desk high with reports, data, and reference material that dated back to Alexander Graham Bell.

"Read it, Lee. Take your time. Give me a short synopsis when you finish your look-see." I said. The mass of printed material I assumed would bury Wildeboar for several weeks. Or perhaps just cause him to chuck it all for a spell at a friendly pub. Meanwhile, the New York market studiers and project planners would be completing his negative report with a small space left on the last page for Wildeboar's endorsement.

A week passed. At odd moments I made it my business to pass Wildeboar's office, noting the little man attacking the research material with vigor, making neat piles of books and exhibits in different parts of the office. I was pleasantly surprised at Wildeboar's professional approach and the seriousness with which he was undertaking the charade. No matter what his revels the night before, he showed up ready for duty each morning and proceeded to his tasks with dispatch. Never mind the occasional shaking hand or green gills or bloodshot eyes, Wildeboar was present and engaged, daily, at the appointed hour.

"That son-of-a-bitch came to play," the controller said, marveling after the Wildeboar reputation that had preceded him. "Are you sure he will go along with whatever you guys are concocting for him?"

"Absolutely. It will take him until well after the report is published to get all those papers he is sorting into neat little piles," I said.

"What papers?" the controller said.

"His filing system. The piles of memos and graphs and

such all over his office. Floor to ceiling. There seem to be three designations for the piles, 'A.B.,' 'E.B.,' and 'O.K.' I'm told they define 'American Bullshit,' 'European Bullshit,' and 'Correct.' As complete a system as I can imagine."

"American Bullshit, eh. What about the Japs?" he said. "They know more about telephones than any of you. Where is the 'Japanese Bullshit' pile?" I remembered I was talking to an accountant and bid him good day.

We assumed Wildeboar would use the opportunity to help out a little here and there, but primarily to feather his nest in the consulting trade. He could squirrel away enough material for three or four years of technical paper writing while on our payroll. He could support himself for years by touring the circuit of international telecommunications conferences, certainly a pleasant way to ease himself into his retirement years. So we ascribed reasonable and selfish motives to his activities, forgot about him, and went on to more pressing matters.

Two weeks to the day of his arrival Wildeboar emerged from his cubbyhole office, lit a cigarette and said, "Well, that's done it. Do you have any more information I should read before I begin?"

"Begin what?" I asked. I thought he was considering starting the cocktail hour at six bells on a bright morning.

"Well, I've digested just about everything that you've given me," Wildeboar said. "And classified it, so to speak. I think it's about time that I began to dash off some recommendations and conclusions. I assume your chaps in New York will be expecting some kind of a report?"

"Yes, of course, I'm sure they will. Our chaps in New

York, yes . . . Well, I suppose you should start your, ah, composition. Do you need any secretarial assistance?"

"Oh, no thank you. I've already had several offers from these kind young ladies about the offices here. I'm sure they'll take care of my requirements. Believe I'll dictate a bit first and see how it goes. Can you arrange for some people to draw curves and graphs?"

I phoned and made arrangements for some graphic people to be assigned to Wildeboar part time. A small suspicion began to gnaw that there might be more from Wildeboar than his signature at the conclusion of our project planning report. I thought about trying to arrange for him to have a heart to heart talk with the general manager so that the facts of life might be gently conveyed. But, what the hell, I thought — what harm in generating a little technical prose on the side? Adroitly plagiarized, some sections might be suitable fodder for a monthly management report at some later date.

During the next few weeks Lee stayed glued to his chair, hunched over the Norelco dictating equipment, confiding to the microphone his innermost thoughts and incisive speculations for hours on end. During office lulls in activity two or three secretaries were always marginally available to him and he kept them stocked with his tapes to transcribe. Somewhere along the line he had learned to operate in this sort of office vacuum, managing to deputize small task forces of temporarily idle office help to assist him. The high stacks in his outgoing basket returned as sheaves of typed copy in very short order. I doffed my bush cap to Welsh ingenuity.

His sheaves of typing soon accumulated into chapters which were punched and placed into notebooks. The notebooks began to fill his bookcases in substantial numbers. Soon additional bookcases were required. And still Wildeboar talked into the Norelco.

This staggering rate of paper production began to concern the general manager.

"My secretary tells me that Wildeboar may have taken to designing a new telephone cable plant, from the look of things," he said. "What the hell is going on? Does he know that he's here to perform a technical audit? He should be working with your market research people. Who the hell is watching him?"

"He wants to write a report. I don't think anyone has made his role clear, so he is proceeding on his own tack. Why don't you have a chat with him?" I said.

"Damn right I will," said the general manager.

But he didn't. And I didn't. And Wildeboar rolled on.

"Somebody should suggest to him that the die may be already cast," the product line manager said at a New York review. "You give your esteemed group vice president a report recommending 20 million dollars more in the ground for a telecommunications cable plant and you've got your head in your hands. And mine. Everyone except Wildeboar will be in deep dung. Straighten him out, now."

So for what it was worth, I approached Wildeboar to learn the results of his research findings, and what might be his intent concerning the disposition of the library he was building.

"You say there is a certain reluctance to invest money in

a telephone cable plant. That's not surprising. But, you see, these staff fellows don't know a great deal about our business, do they? I say, you put up a proper plant here in San Diego and the cable will damn near find its way to the customers. So, that's it, isn't it? Up with the plant and the rest will take care of itself. Providing, of course, that you have some reasonably able commercial people. And I'm sure you do."

At the first news of Wildeboar's defection the general manager was frantic. He paced his office and bemoaned the infidelity of the Welsh. "The cable will find its way to market. We are supposed to ask Geneen for twenty million dollars more for a project to produce a product that is going to creep out the door and up the nearest telephone pole."

"Why the hell didn't you talk to him?" I said. "He thinks he is doing exactly what we ordered. Are you afraid he may quote you to Bennett?"

"You get what you pay for, I guess," the controller said. "What we have here is an engineer on vacation who thinks he has to write us the *How to Build Factories* book to pay for his keep. We should have used the Stanford Research people; then we'd know what to expect."

In spite of the subtle harassments and the gradual withdrawal of secretarial assistance. Wildeboar floundered bravely on. His dictation schedule was still arduous. He spent many hours drafting his own charts and his ability to clip, paste, and arrange graphics was semi-professional. Wildeboar had spun off into his own orbit and seemed to be trying to establish a record for technical report writing.

Now the reams of copy and the notebooks had filled the bookshelves and were overflowing to the tops of tables and his desk and covering the office floor.

"I estimate Mr. Wildeboar's book is longer than *War and Peace* or *Gone With the Wind*," my secretary said. "Pretty soon it will be longer than both. Isn't he a cute little man?"

"What the hell are we going to do?" asked the general manager, mildly frantic. "Who does he think he's writing the report for, assuming he ever finishes it?"

"Don't know. A bit long. But sound," the division engineering manager said. "Some good technical stuff there. Even some innovation. Of course, I haven't finished all of his conclusions —"

"Balls, I don't care about the quality of the goddam thing. He was imported to sign off on our studies. Turn this thing off. I'm not paying him to reinvent the wheel or write me the history of polyethylene extrusion."

"Short of ordering him absolutely to cease and desist, I don't know how the hell you're going to stop him," I said. "Even if you made all the secretaries suddenly unavailable I think he'd find a way. And at this point I don't think we should be obvious. The time to turn him off is past."

"It's certainly going to take a long time to digest all that," the engineering manager chuckled and gummed his pipe. "Something like the Einsteinean equations, if you know what I mean." No one laughed.

For want of a solution, we turned our backs on Wildeboar and allowed his technical stream of consciousness to continue. No one wanted to muzzle him for fear of a leak to Geneen, and no one wanted to support him and risk angering the group veep.

I noticed Wildeboar had managed an ethnic detachment and shunned the Americanization process that our other imported British technicians had taken to so quickly. His watch, incredibly, remained on United Kingdom time; he read the *London Times* a week old and celebrated all the British holidays, whether they agreed with our working schedules or not. His cocktail hours grew longer as he explored San Diego and found some compatible watering holes, but his deportment continued most satisfactory. He was a gentleman, obviously a scholar, and so unpretentious as to blend with the wallpaper. Such people manage anywhere, even in Southern California. Management gradually lost concern about his activities as more pressing problems and the routine catastrophes of plant construction occupied the working hours.

Wildeboar's report grew, and grew, and grew. I would try to lunch with him every week to keep abreast of his progress and disposition. To dissuade him from his labors was hopeless, but I did learn a great deal about the telephone cable business in the process.

Occasionally, the Wildeboar problem would surface at a manager's meeting.

"You know, what the guy is doing is laying down his life for the division. On paper, at least," I said.

"What the hell does that mean?" the general manager asked peevishly. For some reason he seemed to hold me responsible for the Wildeboar thorn in his side. Probably because I delivered him from the airport.

"I suspect that he is summarizing his entire experience in the cable industry on this planet for forty years in those reports. A technical autobiography, of a sort. Not only everything he's learned, discovered, and researched, but every scrap of information he considers in any way useful. Even the trivia he's picked up anywhere along the line. It's all there. I'll bet that if you read the Wildeboar Chronicles in detail, somewhere you'll find handy hints on cable splicing that date back to World War I. Just in case you should dig up a French battlefield some day."

"Look, we must get our recommendations back to New York pretty quickly," the general manager said. "And in some kind of an intelligent conclusion, if we're to oppose the grand plans of top management to locate another plant here. We can't do that reasonably with him still out here scribbling. Some smart ass on the staff is going to want to know what old Lee Wildeboar thinks of the whole thing. So how do we wrap him up?"

"This is like belling the cat," I said. "We have been over this ground before."

"We could have submitted our findings without comment before Wildeboar arrived, but now he has to be heard from." The general manager pounded his desk, "We're pinned down by that goddam report. Somebody has to read it and extract it and at least find out what the hell he is trying to tell us."

"Lee is in technical orbit still," said the engineering manager. "Better wait for his re-entry. What he seems to want us to put together is somewhere between Standard Telephones and the AT and T equipment. It's a tricky technical position, you see, and I don't propose to second-guess it."

There were gestures of dismissal with honor and prizes, but Wildeboar brushed them aside. He would not go home

on company paid vacations to celebrate Guy Fawkes Day
or the National Bank Holidays.

"Duty first, thank you, chaps. Have to stay here and
carry on," Wildeboar said with a touch of Churchill.

Finally, the Wildeboar machine ground to a halt. The
report was complete, volumes arranged, charts corrected,
and a letter of submission prepared. Brave readers who accepted the review assignment were soon lost in the sequence of footnotes, annexes, and abstracts. The technical
saga might be unreadable to most, but it would stand as a
monument for some time as the complete lore on building
cable plants on sandy beaches and bearding the AT&T's and
GTC's in their technological dens. Obviously, there were no
dissenting opinions to his conclusions — none of the reviewers were competent enough to differ with the Wildeboar Chronicles. But even with the report partially digested, from the conclusions the reviewers made available
to us it was obvious Wildeboar was recommending ITT
build a telephone cable plant in San Diego with all dispatch. No doubt about it, that was what Lee Wildeboar
was telling us.

Shortly before the division's project planning report was
due we were visited by the hierarchy. "You can't put this
son-of-a-bitch on the stand in New York," the Defense
Space Group vice president was most emphatic. "If he
thinks that encyclopedia he's writing will put twenty million dollars into the ground here, he's crazy. I won't sign
my name on a recommendation for a nickel more in this
program. The submarine cable plant will never turn a
profit, ever. No way. I can always confess to Geneen that

he was misguided in the first place, and take my chances. But he would never excuse this kind of mistake. It would be a fraud."

We assured him our recommendations and those of the North American staff were harmonious and unanimous in suggesting a delay in new plant construction. But what to do with Wildeboar's report was the question. Should it be refuted, held for study, or simply ignored? We were running out of time.

As far as the vice president was concerned, we would lie. "Just a little truth-stretching, maybe. Say his conclusions are tentative; perhaps a touch negative in some areas, but generally, they agreed with ours. If a telephone cable plant is going to be built, the report may suggest it should be built somewhere else, by some other group in Saint Louis or Kansas City. O.K.? Good. Then we've decided. That's the party line. Get your report ready and we'll schedule a meeting in New York week after next. It may be risky but it's our only out. And please, cut this crazy bastard off and send him on his way with our thanks and a fat consulting fee. Do you understand?"

We understood.

As we were preparing Wildeboar's surprise going-away party, he vanished. The first day he didn't show up at the office we assumed he was celebrating the conclusion of his studies or the Feast of Saint Andrew's Fireball or the Union Jack Turnip Festival. On the second day we became concerned and began calling his local haunts.

"If you've done away with him, you'll be sorry," the operations vice president said to the general manager. "We don't do that sort of thing over here."

His suite at the El Cortez Hotel was inspected but he was not there. Nor had he checked out. Clubs, roadhouses, and cocktail lounges were searched and ITT divisions were alerted in Los Angeles and Orange County. No trace. More out of desperation than with the thought that he might be incarcerated, we contacted the police. Oh yes, a Lee Wildeboar had been detained. An embarrassment involving leaving the scene of the accident after striking several cars. No, he had not asked that anyone be called. He was rather disturbed by the incident and they thought it best to leave him alone. Nice chap, hoped he had a good lawyer. No, he had left their custody and they were not sure what had happened to him. He was scheduled for a court appearance, if we couldn't contact him otherwise.

Only then were we apprised of Wildeboar's driving problems by his British associates. His license had been suspended for an awkward penchant for driving with a slight touch of liquor on his breath and chronically failing the national balloon tests. So, until recently Lee had not driven for some time and not on the right-hand side of the road for some time longer. Unfortunately this excursion had taken him into downtown San Diego where he sideswiped a few parked cars before being run down by a pack of San Diego's finest on motorcycles.

Suffering embarrassment, fatigue, and a touch of homesickness Lee simply had taken off for parts unknown, alone. After a few days he re-emerged, reported aboard, and explained in appropriately sheepish manner the unpleasantness. He was easily persuaded that we could tidy things up if he decided to go home for a spell.

As W. L. P. Wildeboar waved, glass in hand, from the

window of a departing 747 flight for London, we were touched with a pangs of nostalgia along with our sighs of relief.

"He was a good sort. It won't be the same without old Lee," the engineering manager said.

"Christ, let's hope not. Pay all the tabs and bury that report," the general manager said.

"Whose idea was it to call him over here in the first place?" the controller said.

"Shut up." The general manager pushed through the revolving door. "The Wildeboar affair is over."

Up in New Jersey

AFTER TEN WINKS on the American "red eye" 747 flight from Los Angeles to New York and a dash through the wilds of Northern Jersey to the ITT Communications Product Department facilities, I was in poor shape for a pre-summit meeting. But it was Business Plan time again and the Defense Space Group clan was gathering to do their annual thing before Geneen. I arranged my tired bones in a comfortable leather chair and dozed from time to time at the monotonous buzzing of the Communications product boys, droning on through a rehearsal of their reports, scheduled to be presented to Geneen on the morrow. I noted how Bob Chasen, our Defense Space Group father confessor, seemed more and more to resemble Mr. Peepers — plumper and a bit balder, but always fidgeting, smacking his lips, clicking his tongue, while at the same time managing a strained smile. I found Chasen's smile irritating, because it was artificial, but it was a bellwether worth noting. The more Chasen smiled, the worse you knew a situation was growing. Now his smile was from ear to ear and his hands were shaking as they pawed through the papers on the table in front of him. He was obviously not pleased with what he was hearing. He shook his head and muttered, "No, no. It can't be. It just isn't possible." He seemed to be speaking to no one in particular, ignoring the staff member who was midway in his intonation of the litany of group operation results.

Chasen held up a limp hand and motioned me to a chair beside him. The speaker continued, squeaking and growling as the slides slipped by and the lights flickered alternately dimly and brightly in colors on the screen. The Cable Division's Business Plan in a large red notebook, gold-edged, was open before Chasen, liberally paper clipped for reference.

"We are removing some of the sections from your plan. And revising others. The revisions are being run off now. You'll have them in an hour," he said, blinking, smiling, and looking apologetic. "Pretty bad, this whole thing, don't you think?"

"The Business Plan?" I asked.

"Yes — and no. I mean the slide show and animal act we are in the middle of here," Chasen motioned to the stage.

"What's the problem?" I asked.

"It's a lousy year. Profits are down, prospects are bad. The poor bastards are trying to make a recession look like a rosy boom. They'll never make it."

He drummed his fingers on our Business Plan, lying open to the sales projection curves. He peeked up at me through thin eyelashes, nodding and smiling. "Aren't you curious about the revisions?"

"Whatever is right. It strikes me as a bit late though. And where did the new information come from?" I asked. "And for that matter, where the hell are my two partners in crime?" The general manager and controller had agreed to rendezvous with me at Chasen's office. They were nowhere to be seen.

Chasen looked blankly at the animation on the screen for a long few seconds, then said, "They called to say that Moore and Binks couldn't make it."

"Who called? Did Moore and Binks call?" I was stunned. The absence of two of the three senior division managers from the annual Business Plan Review was unthinkable. It was like defecting on the eve of battle or sneaking out of the ring before the first bell.

"Our humble and winsome new group vice president called," Chasen said. "He said to put on the show without them, Moore and Binks can't make it."

"You are joking, Bob. Because unless they have both been cashiered out of hand this very day these two have a responsibility for a large part of the document under your hand. And some of the parts I don't care to try to explain at all," I said.

Chasen shrugged, "New York said they wouldn't be here. What the hell can I do?"

"There's a rat to be smelled here, obviously. For those two to absent themselves from this soirée voluntarily would involve some kind of a suicide pact. And believe me, neither of them is the type," I said.

"Perhaps. But someone called the group offices from New York and said that they would not be here for the meeting — period. Apparently it is left for you and me to stand in for them and present the Cable Division Business Plan, such as it is."

"Such as it is, is well put. Since you have apparently reviewed the financial projections your willingness to be booked into this act is a show of great courage," I said.

Chasen noticed that his staff was now quiet, their attention focused on our conversation. He signaled me to silence.

"We'll discuss this later," he said. The meeting lasted fifteen minutes and broke up with harried staff members hurrying out in all directions to make eleventh hour changes to their slides and charts. Chasen led me to a small room adjoining his office where the Cable Division exhibits had been mounted and taped to the walls for final review and a check on the graphics. It was obvious, even on cursory examination, that the sales and profit projections had been considerably altered from those my marketing people had developed.

"I believe that I begin to see the proportions of the problem," I said. "Someone has managed to change all of the numbers from tragedy to comedy. These are all very pretty. I like the black figures better than the red ones, anyway. They are sure to please Geneen a hell of a lot more."

"Since our humble and winsome new group vice president called and suggested that we two put on the show I thought you should have an opportunity to review all this." Chasen gestured to the chart covered walls.

"Thank you. I note someone has taken liberties with our sales figures as well. In fact, the whole goddam thing is different. Everything goes up, up, and away. Apparently someone has received a visitation from on high, or a war has been declared or, more likely, someone is kidding all of us." I traced the five-year sales curve up over the $100 million division. "You do realize, don't you, that this is pure, unadulterated horse manure, Grade One A. And this information conflicts with every report submitted by the Cable Division for the past six months."

Chasen fell into the chair and drummed his fingers on the table. He looked shaken, and now his grin was ghastly.

"Someone on high in New York decided not to use the data in the plan you submitted. We got the word a few days ago to go in with the figures about the same as last year's projections. I thought Moore and Binks would be here to explain," he said.

"Well, that accounts for the absence of our two erstwhile fellow travelers. It would be difficult to grill them tomorrow by long distance phone. But they'll have to stand behind this plan sometime, I assume. Or can you vacate responsibility completely simply by going on French leave?"

"The word is not to do anything to rock the boat. Keep all the numbers happy ones, I've been told. This head-in-the-sand attitude is not my idea," Chasen said. "But what the hell can I do?"

"What, indeed." On that note, we adjourned until dinner.

There was a great plot hatching, obviously, but these corporate intrigues were impossible to piece together until the power play was made. Chasen was the man caught in the middle, trying to keep his own position reasonably secure without antagonizing his boss or playing the fool before Geneen.

We had dinner in one of the posh steak houses near the

plant in Ho-Ho-Kus, Chasen and his staff ate with all the gusto of condemned men at a last candlelight meal. As an old and honored customer, Chasen commanded the very best — great wine, steaks perfectly done, and some special touches of service reserved for minor royalty. But the staff's forced joviality was enough to make the meal a total bust. Except for an occasional weak witticism the conversation was unrelieved shop talk, the kind that curdles the digestion and curbs the appetite. Dinner quickly over, we left to resume the meetings at Chasen's office.

While Chasen busied himself with the other group presentations, I examined the changes made in our Business Plan. I tried to adjust myself to the realization that these were fabrications, misleading propaganda in a format I had grown to respect as mathematically precise. I wondered how Chasen would fare on the witness stand before Chairman Geneen, presenting a plan that he knew was a turkey. I recalled George Banino's verbal flogging at the hands of the staff at the last Business Plan Meeting of the Defense Space Group. I wondered if Chasen could stand up to the lions as well as George had. But even Banino might have trouble with the script of a fairy tale.

Finally Chasen joined me for a two-man rehearsal.

"What do you say when someone pulls out one of our recent reports, Bob? Or has someone put all that information in a shredder?" I said.

"The sales projections were low, very low indeed," Chasen said. "Some people in New York may feel that we need a little time to recoup, if you know what I mean."

"Not to worry, Bob — I'm certainly not going to stand up before Geneen and read a minority report. But to put it simply, we have made some rather serious errors in running the facility at San Diego. We simply can't make all the types of cable we originally projected as product lines."

Chasen fidgeted, "You can't sell from an empty cart. Either you get a larger cart or settle for a smaller part of the business. Is that what you're telling me?"

He was holding me off with platitudes. But the facts were published and easily researched. My conscience was clear, it would bu intorosting to sit through Chasen's presentation — so long as I was not called upon for support.

Chasen began to pace in a short circle behind his chair. "You may be right, you know. But right now we have our orders. It's a matter of timing. Our bosses don't think we can hit Geneen across the face with a wet fish and expect to do anything but cause a goddam riot. Maybe they know some way to pump a few million more into the division's coffers on the sly. Geneen is up to his ass in antitrust problems right now; he may just ignore our little part of the empire for a while."

"And if he doesn't?" I said.

Chasen shrugged. "But who lives forever in this business. Come to my retirement banquet, you're invited — if we bust tomorrow. I can only play it straight. I'll give the Cable Division a few minutes at the end of my presentation. Not more than ten, short and sweet. If Geneen and the staff bore in I'll have to turn it over to you."

"Thank you," I said. "And I'll break into a buck-and-wing and sing 'The Good Ship Lollypop.' "

Chasen smiled broadly, "That will be nice. Tap dance your way out the door to the elevator and I'll meet you there."

Back at the motel I knew that sleep was a long way off. I piled the reports and exhibits on the desk and began the painstaking process of marginal notation. The Business Plan Review reminded me of studying for an open book examination: no matter how many references you toted into the examination room you never seemed to have what was needed to answer the questions. Finally, about four o'clock in the morning, the adrenalin shut off, and I was tired enough to pass out. I slept fitfully and awoke still bone-tired. I recalled snatches of dream in which the Great Ape Kong, looking very much like Geneen, was batting two wing airplanes out of the air from his perch atop the Empire State Building.

It was two in the afternoon and we were sitting in the Business Plan Meeting Room, chilled and apprehensive, looking across the carpeted "great divide," and reading the name plates on the opposite table: Geneen, Dunleavy, Bennett, Westfall . . . We were at a recess, the assembled forty or fifty managers marking time until Geneen and the top brass re-entered. Waiting for Geneen was not like waiting for Lefty, or Godot, or even the jury to return with the verdict. It seemed as though time simply stopped, everyone stood firm in position and nothing happened until he returned. But his managers would rather wait any amount of time for his return than continue without him; the occasional sessions supervised by executive vice presidents did not count. When Geneen was absent the sessions became deflated, routine business discussions where no final decision could be made.

"Have you got everything ready?" Chasen asked me.

I nodded in the affirmative, not knowing what he meant. The melancholy reports that lay in my brief case in front of me were not to be presented, apparently. And I had no market or technical data that would support the presentation Chasen was about to make. But why press poor Robert any further, I thought; what he needs at this time is assurance.

Chasen spoke in a hoarse whisper to the members of his staff flanking him. "This recess means there's going to be a goddam witch hunt. Be sure to get those secondary slides ready in case there are questions. And, please, don't get them out of order. No screw-ups, do you understand?"

The Defense Space Group staff men scurried back and forth in the arena between the tables — distributing supplements, arranging samples, and setting up projectors. Managers who had passed through their ordeal already were now backbenching or enjoying coffee and chatting with an air of relief. It was apparent who had been at bat and who was still in the on-deck circle.

I noticed our ex-group boss Maurie Valente had not left his seat at the great table to recess with Geneen. He was conferring with his staff lieutenants and directing emissaries around the room with messages. One of them approached us and delivered a confidential dispatch to Chasen.

"Maurie says that if there are any questions, he'll help out. I mean, he plans to comment on the great job being done in San Diego. Just give him a lead when things seem logical or if the going gets rough. Understand?"

Chasen nodded stiffly. But with friends like Valente, who needed senior executive type enemies?

Finally, Geneen emerged from the wings with the hierarchy following in order at a respectful distance. All the managers scurried for their chairs, spilling coffee and filling trash containers with half-consumed Danish. Arm in arm with Geneen was a plump little man, conservatively dressed with a sad smile who looked very familiar. Seeing him in this theatre of the absurd was like seeing him walk on stage at the Metropolitan in a Pagliacci costume. The incongruity of the situation struck me and I began to chuckle most inappropriately. Chasen was horror stricken, probably thinking I was parting at the seams.

I was struck not only by the entrance of this player not on the program, but by how much he resembled Geneen in physical appearance and manner. Geneen had him by the arm and was introducing him to a small circle of senior executives and vice presidents around the table.

They all paid him the homage due a Geneen guest. Maurie Valente and Rand Araskog were singled out by Geneen and they carried the conversation until Geneen signaled for the proceedings to begin.

Chasen stared at the visitor, then switched his microphone off, a look of dawning recognition on his face.

"Is that who I think it is?" Chasen said. "Is that Congressman Wilson of San Diego?"

"The same. Congressman Bob, our native son," I said.

"This is unheard of. In twenty years of coming to these things I've never seen a politician in this room during Business Plan presentations."

"Well, you've seen one now." I said. "I assure you, he's a politician, and there he is beside Geneen."

Wilson gave me a nod of recognition, smiled and executed a short wave. We San Diego boys must stick together, he seemed to be saying. With a glow of parochial pride I returned the greeting. He seemed relaxed and self-assured, as though he were addressing a Rotary Club or about to break a bottle at a navy yard christening. Just another performance for the master showman, I thought, today a corporation meeting, tomorrow a flower show.

"What the hell shall we do? Shall I go on with this?" Chasen asked me. "What does he know about the program in San Diego?"

Chasen was crushing my arm in what felt like a death grip. "What the hell else did you have in mind at this point? What difference does it make if Wilson is here or not?" I said.

"Is there some purpose for his being here? I mean listening to this plan? I mean, what could he have told Geneen?" Chasen certainly was one anxious little fellow.

"Don't worry," I said. "This program couldn't have a stronger supporter than Wilson. His information is usually direct from our old pal Dita Beard. Don't clutch; I'm sure Wilson is only interested in the happy stories you're going to tell about employment and investment."

Geneen waved his hand for our dog-and-pony show to begin. Chasen tottered to his feet, took the rostrum, and amid flickering slides began to tell his tale. When he reached the Cable Division part of his presentation he faltered. The cable data slides were as garish as anything

I'd seen; I assumed they had been prepared under Valente's direction. Chasen was having trouble with his voice, it simply wouldn't respond; but the slides kept flipping and they achieved a kaleidoscope effect, impressive enough by itself. When Chasen resumed executing a hoarse croak nothing seemed to have been missed, although he wisely omitted the text that went with the slides and consequently half of his presentation.

Geneen and Wilson sat quietly, attentive to what Chasen was saying in his stumbling fashion. Wilson seemed bored, his glance strayed around the room. It was unusual to see someone sitting so casual and relaxed next to Geneen in the seat of power.

Chasen concluded and I imagined I could feel an electric charge go around the room. The staff began shuffling papers and bringing reports out of their briefcases and we would shortly know whether they had been warned off or instructed to give us a thorough grilling. This would be their once-a-year opportunity to probe the mysteries surrounding the huge ITT investment in the San Diego cable project. It was an irresistible temptation that no staff man would let pass, unless muzzled by Geneen. Chasen concluded with a half stiff bow, his knuckles white as he gripped the podium. He slumped, and his voice was all but gone — but he had toughed it through, to his credit. Bennett rose and turned slowly to Geneen and asked for questions. Geneen leaned over his microphone and we knew that the signal — thumbs up or down — was about to be given.

"Thank you Bob," Geneen said. "Quite an interesting presentation." He turned neither to the right nor to the left to solicit any comment or questions from the staff. He asked a few general questions concerning all of the divisions Chasen had discussed except the Cable Division, then thanked Chasen again and signaled for Bennett to go on with the meeting.

Caught aback, Bennett did a remarkable thing: he tried to lead Geneen.

"Did we cover the Cable Division?" Bennett said. Then it struck him — Geneen was sitting with Congressman Wilson and perhaps had ignored the San Diego project intentionally. A death-like hush fell over the room as the audience realized Bennett's faux pas.

Geneen smiled and turned to Wilson and nodded, then back to Bennett.

"No, I don't think so. The Cable Division has its work cut out for it. Neither Bob nor I have any questions, thank you."

With that, Geneen rose and escorted Wilson toward one of the meeting room exits, signaling that the meeting would again be recessed. He motioned for Araskog, Valente, and two other executives to join him.

And so it was over. The matter of the Cable Division had been dealt with on a higher level, obviously. Perhaps Geneen had adopted a "go easy" philosophy to help indoctrinate the new group vice president and to avoid embarrassing us in front of Wilson. More likely, discussions had been held with Wilson in secret chambers, and Geneen was not in the mood for a public airing. The San Diego project was still in the area of a political sugar plum, I guessed, and not to be bruised by too much jostling.

"We ducked the goddam bullet," Chasen was incredulous. He looked like a man who had been reprieved from the gallows. "But why? Just because that Congressman was here?"

"Wilson once told me that Geneen offered to make him the czar of the hotelkeepers in Southern California," I said. "Maybe he's decided to accept the offer. Probably his visit was social."

"I didn't even think the President of the United States could get into one of these meetings. Congratulations on your choice of California politicians," Chasen said.

"Thanks," I said. "I voted a straight Democrat ticket."

Better Shred

As I READ Jack Anderson's reprint of Dita's memo to Bill Merriam I recalled some of her wilder antics during that previous dangerous summer. What we took as Dita addled by the political heat and pressures of her private antitrust vendetta was really an attempt to wrap the whole thing up for Geneen with little or no assistance from her fellow lobbyists. "Look Hal, no hands!"

Her memo began in low gear.

"I just had a long talk with E.J.G."

Conversations with Gerrity were difficult for Dita, something like chatting with a Mafioso that someday may hold your contract.

"I'm so sorry that we got that call from the White House. I thought you and I had agreed very thoroughly that under no circumstances would anyone in this office discuss with anyone our participation in the convention, including me."

Dita was always the heroine and prime mover of the memos she authored. "Ma" Beard, the mastermind of the sinister affair.

"Other than permitting John Mitchell, Ed Reinecke, Bob Haldeman, and Nixon (besides Wilson, of course) *no one* has known from whom that 400 thousand commitment had come."

No one except a gaggle of ITT top brass and the select of the San Diego business community and reporters for the *San Diego Union, Washington Post, New York Times*, and Republican wheel horses without number.

"You can't imagine how many queries I've had from 'friends' about this, and I have in each and every case denied knowledge of any kind. It would be wise for all of us to continue to do that, regardless of from whom any questions come; White House or whoever. John Mitchell has certainly kept it on the higher level only, we should be able to do the same.

"I was afraid the discussion about the three hundred/ four hundred thousand commitment would come up soon. If you remember, I suggested that we all stay out of that, other than the fact that I told you I heard Hal upped the original amount."

Checking the dates, I wondered if the memo could have been typed by my secretary in San Diego. Dita borrowed her when in town during that period because she was a good typist, new with the company and naive.

"Now I understand from Ned that both you and he are upset about the decision to make it 400 in *services*.

"Believe me, this is not what Hal said. Just after I talked with Ned, Wilson called me to report on his meeting with Hal. Hal at no time told Wilson that our donation was to be in services ONLY."

The fact that services were promoted over cash indicated the public relations man opted for the easily concealed bucks — while the politicians wanted the cash, thanks. You couldn't buy some things with services. Like groceries and the rent. Services were easier to rationalize than the cash without earmarks, and so the cold-feet brigade was holding out for cover. But not Cash-on-the-Barrelhead Dita.

"In fact, quite the contrary. There would be very little cash involved, but certainly some. I am convinced, because of several conversations with Louie re Mitchell, that our noble commitment has gone a long way toward our negotiations on the mergers coming out as Hal wants them. Certainly, the president has told Mitchell to see that things are worked out fairly. It is still only McLaren's mickey-mouse we are suffering.

"We all know Hal has a big mouth! But this is one time he cannot tell you and Ned one thing and Wilson (and me) another!"

Dita was hanging in there. One of the big four with Geneen and Gerrity and Wilson who would ram the settlement through.

"I hope, dear Bill, that all this can be reconciled between Hal and Wilson — if all of us in the office remain totally ignorant of any commitment ITT has made to anyone. If it gets too much publicity, you can believe our negotiations with Justice will wind up shot down. Mitchell is definitely helping us, but cannot let it be known. Please destroy this, huh?"

The plea to destroy the memo was not worthy of Dita; she had seldom expressed so much personal caution. The "negotiations winding up shot down," however, was authentic Dita jargon.

By the time Dita's memo was drafted, most of the machinery was already in operation for ITT to subsidize, supervise, and publicize a Richard M. Nixon style convention in San Diego. To a student of Dita's style the memo appeared authentic — it looked like just one more effort to be sure that she was still on the bandwagon, even if hanging off the tailgate. Her ploy was to let the big boys know that she was "in the know" and should be credited with at least an assist, whatever the outcome of the San Diego adventure. Dita, name-dropper extraordinaire, was in top form in drafting the memo; it included eight important names from ITT and the Republican Administration, from Nixon to Reinecke via Wilson and Louie Nunn. Certainly better than par for a page-and-a-half memorandum.

As the affair was breaking in the press and Dita was winging her way west to Colorado, Charley Farwell called from the Cable Division chambers within the ITT Washington Office. He was in a state of high excitement.

"I am sitting in the middle of a goddam paper-shredding ceremony of monumental proportion," he said. "Best thing that ever happened to this outfit. The security boys from New York took all our goddam files and shredded them up in these ingenious machines. I immediately wrote a memo renouncing responsibility for anything that's happened in this office during the past two years."

"Have any of Dita's friends or lieutenants been around?" I asked.

"The New York Mafioso came down in force and made

sure that Dita was gone, together with everything that she owned. They took her pictures off the office wall, they may be removing the wallpaper now. It's incredible how badly this witch hunt is being handled."

"Do you remember the scrap of history Dita lost in the Washington bistro while she was with us?" I asked. "Her notes from the White House on the antitrust case. Think of all the money we could have made selling short. I don't think we took dear Dita seriously enough."

"Bet your ass we didn't," Charlie said. "All the smart bastards in New York either sold out or borrowed on the family jewels and took a short position. Anyway, there are two versions of the real story making the rounds."

"Official and unofficial? Memo correct and memo faked?"

"No. Everybody allows that the information and memo is correct," Charlie said. "The big question is how Anderson picked up the precious document. One version is that there is a spy in the office exporting this stuff to Anderson, and maybe others. Most people don't buy that, at least not a secret agent of any great abilities. The other is that Dita got tired of playing up to Gerrity and the New York crew. She felt that her neck was in the noose anyway, so she cheated the hangman and evened up some old debts with her enemies within the ranks. And made sure that Anderson picked up a copy of the memo, knowing she would be protected once the word was out."

"That's the one I believe," I said, "that she fixed the bastards, but good."

"Who can say? Some of us don't have Dita's political

imagination. But there's a hell of a lot more going on here than Dita's memo spells out. I'm just as glad they're shredding the files and plans in our office as well as the others. From now on I write on nothing but easily digested rice paper."

"Well, as they say over bugged telephones — so long till next time." I said. "Keep the faith and your sense of humor as long as possible."

"Goodbye from Never Never Land," Charley said. "See you in the funny papers."

In many ways the discovered memo was Dita's ultimate victory, her chance to be somebody in a big political scheme, a position that no electorate or corporation or political party would ever have bestowed on her. Her pictures in the *New York Times* and her biography in *Time* magazine, interviewed on television, sought after by Senate committees, she was, at last, the Ms. National Celebrity she had always yearned to be. I was delighted for her hour of glory. She certainly had labored long in the salt mines for it.

I decided I'd remove some of the intimate little notes from Dita in my confidential files for sure preservation. My favorite was a particularly pungent missive in which she demanded we hire Doctor Liskas' unemployed son, who could only work engineering problems in broken Hungarian but would be useful "building your cable stuff." If Dita ever decided on or was pushed into really telling the ITT story her memos would certainly be worth a fortune in my grandchildren's time.

Conclusion

"WE THINK a philosophy of varied industries can lead to a more efficient corporate vehicle than the traditional pattern and one, moreover, that develops management capabilities and flexibilities that no one industry approach can provide." So says Geneen, the Shadow of ITT, from atop his Park Avenue redoubt.

Perhaps so. But many question where the multinational conglomerate movement is leading us — especially when that movement is orchestrated and played by ITT.

. . . are Geneen and his ilk the new robber barons with sinister international ambitions?

. . . has the free enterprise system become a freak-out kind of capitalism wherein only the welfare of the company is primary?

. . . is patriotism gradually shifting worldwide to multinational companies?

. . . is what is best for the company always best for the country — or the world, for that matter?

There is certainly plenty of evidence available to suggest that the conglomerates, both multinational and domestic, have found ways to ignore the old laws of the free market place. But as laissez-faire philosophers suggest, perhaps the system is moribund anyway. As the tank and bomber put an end to sanity and personal involvement in warfare, so the assembly line and computer may have already put an end to the possibility of an equitable system of business competition — and further, personal job satisfaction. We are told that soon the technicrats will join with the new breed of corporation executive to usher in the dawn of the model industrial state wherein the large multinational corporations become the keepers of the prosperity of the world. And the signs are there, even now. It appears that nations of the world are slowly slipping into an economic anarchy and the largest and most powerful companies are adopting a sort of de facto statehood — beyond control, regulation, and, in some cases, positive national identification. This trend is ominous to those who understand the philosophy of the corporate giants. It is natural for patriotism to shift from the countries to the corporations. There are some startling recent examples of the foul play, cravenness, and clandestine and illegal behavior by the managements of companies whose powers governments have threatened to investigate or curtail. Those who are not with the company are against the company and acknowledged enemies. And management loyalty remains with the company. Of that there is little doubt.

As Nixon moves precariously along in his second term and the disaster of Watergate spreads, the relationship between big business and government is also coming under closer scrutiny. There is an uneasy feeling in the land that economic power is too concentrated. The role of the giant corporation in American society is being re-evaluated and redefined, hopefully toward achieving some more effective means of regulation. And the multinational conglomerate, that even less understood corporate entity, is being viewed with mounting suspicion as the successor to the international cartel system that flourished before World War II

So we are left with this question: are the multinational corporate giants the buccaneers and villains of the world economy who subvert the countries in which they are in residence or are they a new breed of advanced business practitioner who will finally make the trains run on time? Hopefully, the stories in this book will help to give you an insight into the world of ITT and some basis for judgment of it. Perhaps they will stimulate your interest to learn more about the corporate giants and conglomerates, the multinationals and their chiefs and supporters. These men and their companies, for better or worse, are rapidly changing your world.

Since these tales must end somewhere, probably Dita Beard's denouement and the period of the rapacious ITT shredder will do, for now. But one more story before we close. It is a Geneen Fable, of course, about Mr. Geneen and his Business Machine. As in most tales it is difficult to decide whether he plays antagonist or protagonist. But no matter, if Geneen had enough arms and legs and time, he would play all the characters in all the stories in that fairyland known as ITT.

On a hectic tour of international negotiating, Geneen himself and entourage dropped into the Washington office on short notice. Geneen told Bill Merriam that he would have time to have lunch with the British Ambassador and to ring the Ambassador up and inform him. The Ambassador quickly agreed but was held up by crosstown traffic and consequently delayed. As the clock hand slipped a minute past the appointed meeting time Geneen displayed some disgust at the tardiness, picked up the *Washington Post* and left for the men's room, announcing that he would not be back before he had finished the sports page. The Ambassador arrived a few minutes later, out of breath and full of apologies. It fell to Bill Merriam to let him know that he was in for a bit of heel cooling. Merriam's turn of phrase became a company classic.

"Mr. Ambassador, please make yourself comfortable. I'm afraid we're in for a short wait," Merriam said. "Mr. Geneen is engaged in the only activity with which none of us can assist him."

Perhaps by describing his company and his international system, by humanizing some of his managers, by relating the misadventures, heroics, and bumblings of some of his resident characters and clowns I have reversed the situation Bill Merriam described. These tales may have done for Mr. Geneen what he could not do for himself.